#beyondwords

An Anthology

Written by
The 2014-2015 Freshman Class

Maryville Junior High School

Title, *#beyondwords*, conceived by Lauren Hamby.

Cover artwork in pen and watercolor by Haley Kratz.

Cover design consultation by Brandon Everett.

Proofreading provided by retired English teacher Donna K. Cantrell.

Compiled and edited by MJHS Computer Applications instructors Sherri B. McCall and Jody C. Dyer.

This work was created, compiled, produced, and published solely for educational purposes. Along with haiku, students used Twitter.com's concept of hashtags, variations of the *Six Word Memoir*, historically credited to Ernest Hemingway, and instructional templates to create personal versions of the original 1993 poem, titled "Where I'm From" by writer and teacher, George Ella Lyon, as well as original pieces of work.

ISBN 13: 978-0692308189
ISBN 10: 0692308180

For more information on the project, please email Jody C. Dyer at jody.dyer@maryville-schools.org or Sherri B. McCall at sherri.mccall@maryville-schools.org.

Foreword
By author Dr. Lin Stepp

Writing—and the writing of poetry—can stimulate imagination and expand the vocabulary and the creative thinking quotient of young people. It introduces the young—and the old—to rhythm and rhyme and to figurative speech, creating a greater sensitivity to language. According to Aguilar, "poetry promotes literacy, builds community, and fosters emotional resilience."

As a young girl, I wrote poetry, especially in my teens and early adult years. When I was a young child, my mother—who loved poetry—read poems of all kinds and types to me to such an extent that I can still quote many large sections of the poems we read together today. I think hearing, reading, and writing poetry when young helped to shape my feel for the beauty of the written word, helped me see and feel the cadence and flow of sound and to realize how words, just of themselves when well-chosen, could create visual pictures.

Today I am an author with Kensington Publishing of New York. I have best-selling and international titles—and I am grateful for the rich background in literature and poetry I gained through my early home life and through my teachers at school. Some of my first "recognized" pieces of writing were poems my teachers put on the class bulletin board or included in school publications.

Because of how richly I value the teaching of poetry and creative writing in the classroom, I was pleased when Jody Dyer asked me to write a foreword to this book of student works. I am also an educator, still certified for elementary and middle school teaching, but now teaching research and psychology at the college level. In my postsecondary courses, I encourage my students to write—and to appreciate writing and to strengthen their writing skills—and it is an honor to have a celebratory part in this fine student effort.

It was a joy to read the fine poems in this collection, based in part on Appalachian author George Ella Lyon's work and her poetry style in the poem "Where I'm From." Lyon once said, 'I believe when we write, or practice any of the creative arts, that we're listening to our hearts and expressing what we hear.' I think you will find that these student poems and writings well reflect those words.

Dr. Lin Stepp

Author of the Smoky Mountain novels including *Down by the River* (June, 2014) and *Makin' Miracles* (January, 2015) and co-author with J.L. Stepp of *The Afternoon Hiker* (February, 2014)

Author's website: www.linstepp.com

Introduction

During the fall of the 2014-2015 academic year, Maryville Junior High School (MJHS) ninth grade Computer Applications students completed a comprehensive assignment called the "Student Anthology Project." This highly technical, cross-curricular, multi-day lesson addressed numerous Computer Applications, English I, Marketing I, Family Consumer Science, and Teen Living Tennessee State Standards in a meaningful way.

Students worked individually and collaborated with teachers and peers to compose, proofread, edit, design, and finally publish their original creative work in the form of this printed anthology. We (Sherri B. McCall and Jody C. Dyer) would like to thank the following faculty members, who, with great enthusiasm and professional insight, guided students through important sections of the Student Anthology Project:

Janice Cates, Community Relations Specialist
Julie Drake, Art Instructor
Brynn Everett, Family and Consumer Science Instructor
Rosanna Giles, Marketing Instructor
Lisa McGinley, Principal of Maryville Junior High School

We would also like to thank the parents of our ninth grade authors for encouraging their children to embrace this project and see it all the way through to an exciting end — a "real world" product in which they should take great academic pride.

Jody C. Dyer and Sherri B. McCall

#beyondwords

An Anthology

Written by
The 2014-2015 Freshman Class

Maryville Junior High School

Dalton

I am from riding dirt bikes on I-40
From KTM, and pick-up soccer games at the park
I am from out in the middle of nowhere, the sticks
I am from the honeysuckle and the ladybug tree in the front yard
From not having big birthday parties and staying up late on the
weekends
DeLaras and Langdons
I am from being really short or really tall and having a short
temper
From "Don't let the bed bugs bite" and "Don't get out of bed
again or the night monsters will get you"
I am from "Who needs God's house to pray in when you can talk
to Him in your own house?"
I'm from Poughkeepsie, New York
An Italian and German background
From lasagna and sauerkraut
From the time I broke a window with a soccer ball
From when my dad handed me a lacrosse stick when I was one
and said, "Here, catch!"
I am from family heirlooms stuck in the attic for years to come
And my mom still taking pictures

Tommy

I am from Nutella

From Mayfield and Windex

I am from the average house on an average street

Walled, air conditioned

It looked like a house

I am from the rock

The hickory tree

Tall, dropping nuts everywhere

I'm from the huge Thanksgivings

From shortness

From Luke and Sarah and Susan

I'm from talking really loud and walking really fast

I'm from "Good job" and "Have a good day!"

I'm from Iowa and Europe

From hamburgers and steak

From the time my ancestors crossed a boat to America

The blue eyes in the box in the attic

I'm from the house on Young Avenue

George

I'm from shirts
From Nike and Head
I'm from the wood of the floor brown, yellow
It sounded creaky
I'm from Rosemary, Lavender whose leaves smell so fresh
I'm from the bread and the laughter from Pete and Pamela and
George
I'm laughter and joking
From "Do not lie" to "Eat all your food"
I'm from Christianity and God
I'm from Tennessee and gyro and feta cheese
From the uncle whose pants fall down and the uncle who sings
I'm from Tennessee
I'm from a great funny family

Six Word Story

George

Maryville Rebels always beat Bearden Bulldogs

Aiden

I'm from oranges
From charcoal and Adidas
I'm from the Bible Belt
Happiness and opportunity
It was ordinary
I'm from the foot, the powerful shoe
I'm from the ball and good aim
From Matt and Alyssia and Yoda
I'm from the smoke and strictness
From "Man up" and "Grow up"
I'm from Christianity
I'm from Florida
Cabbage and pot roast
From the captain
The Great Naples
I'm from hilarious people

Maryville High School New Fight Song

Aiden

Oh! We are the red and black!

Of the mighty Rebels!

We always win!

Look out! Look out!

Here come the mighty, mighty red and black!

No. No. We can't lose!

Who? Who? (fast)

No! We can't be stopped!

Ah, Ah! (fast)

We win! (fast) We win! (fast)

Now once again!

No! No. We can't be stopped!

Joseph

I am from Marucci bats

From baseball and Nike

I am from dirt roads, dusty back roads

It feels like a blanket of filth

I am from mountains and hills

Large

I'm from Italian ancestry

From Clare and Bob and Hope

I'm from the loud and competitive

From a pro baseball player, adopted

I'm from Catholic churches and Italy

Pizza and pasta

From the grandfather who fought in Vietnam and the

grandmother who cooks

I am from Maryville, Tennessee

Bailey

I'm from crayons
From Clorox and Play-Doh
I'm from the sweetest people
Banjos, rocking
It feels warm
I'm from the dandelions,
The sweet smelling dandelions, tall and yellow
I'm from cabin camping and being short in height
From Jason and Jessica and Carol
I'm from the crazy and the loving
From Santa Claus and the Tooth Fairy
I'm from Christianity
The Bible
I'm from Tennessee
Greenville and Bristol
From the dad who played a bunch of pranks on our whole family
The skinny majorettes
Pictures, high and low, on tables and walls
I'm from Maryville, where football and grades are everything

Cora

I'm from the washing machine

From Dove soap and Johnson's baby powder

I'm from the house at the end of the road

Clean and small, it felt warm

I'm from the strawberry plants

And the sunflower

Big, bright and yellow

I'm from family reunions in Cades Cove and green eyes

From Candie and Glenn

And Camden

I'm from the laughing and arguing about the rain being God's

tears

From dogs on the roof

I'm from "Hallelujah, hallelujah"

And "Praise the Lord"

I'm from Maryville, Tennessee

Mashed potatoes and fried chicken

From the times when my Papaw would tell me stories

The crazy dog lady

Crooked, upside down

I'm from a small town atmosphere found at the foothills of the

Great Smoky Mountains, mostly pronounced "Murville"

I am a person with a lot of thoughts

Hashtag Poem

Cora

#im #not #dead
#but #im #not #alive
#im #not #living
#im #just #trying #to #survive

Caroline

I am from books
From candles and dogs
I am from the mountains, tall and beautiful, they look like giants
I am from dogwoods and iris, beautiful and purple
I'm from horse rides and green eyes
From Belinda and John and Jack
I'm from the love of my parents
From the knowledge of my family
From the tooth fairy and the Easter bunny
I'm from Methodist Church and Sunday school
I'm from Chattanooga and Ireland
Meat and potatoes
From the story of the time my parents got married
And the time I got stuck upside down on a swing set
From the family photo albums
I am from the love of my family and the curiosity of the world

Ale

I am from hot Cheetos

From Crest toothpaste and the BP station

I am from the land of the mountains, big and tall

They looked beautiful

I am from the dark yellow daises, the rose bushes

They filled up the yard

I'm from the quincenerias and brown eyes

From Carmen and Jesus

I'm from Christmas dinners and huge family breakfasts

From "The monster will get you if you act bad" and "Save your tooth for the Tooth Fairy"

I'm from, "Jesus died for our sins," and "Jesus loves you"

I'm from Tennessee, home of the Volunteers

Sweet tea and buttered biscuits

From the four-wheeler that ran over my sister

And the bike my big sister flipped over to hurt her leg

The pictures that hang in the living room and all over the shelves

I am from a happy, wonderful family

Emily

I am from dress up and makeup

From outside and cookouts

I am from the brick walls

Safe and sturdy

They felt like sand paper

I am from the flowers in the garden

The playhouse in the backyard

Old and scary

I'm from vacations and brown hair

From Darryll and Janie and Natalie

I'm from late night dinners and people laughing

From "You can be anything you want to be" and "Never give up

on what you started"

I'm from singing in church every Sunday

The passages the preacher read that changed my life

I'm from Maryville, Tennessee

Sweet tea and Coca-Cola

From losing every game we play on Christmas

The crazy dancing

From the chairs and yelling to hurry up

I am from an amazing family with many memories

Letter to Future Self

Madison

Dear Madison,

You are one heck of a student. You crack a lot of jokes and you are a crazy and wild friend. But, you are a great student and work hard in class. I love you as a student, but you still need to study more. I would love to see you succeed and graduate as a doctor or lawyer. I think, as your younger self, you can do it if you just work a little harder. If you just listen to me you will be successful.

Elias

I'm from clothespins

From Clorox

I am from the dirt under the back porch

I'm from the forsythia bush

And the Dutch elm

I'm from fudge and eyeglasses

From Imogene and Alafair

I'm from the know-it-alls and pass-it-ons

From "Perk up!" and "Pipe down."

I'm from restoring my soul with a cotton ball lamb and ten
verses

From the finger my grandfather lost to an auger and the eye my
father shut to keep his sight

Under my bed, a dress box spilling old pictures, a sift of lost
faces to drift beneath my drams

I am from those moments—snapped before I budded—a leaf to
fall from the family tree

Kerrigan

I am from Rip Curl
From surfboards and rash guards
I am from the board shavings on my front porch (scratchy and painful but it's who I am)
 I am from the ocean in my backyard
It was salty but smelled like home to me
I am from dandelions, blowing swiftly through the winds
I'm from the chicken hunt and Margaretville
From 100 and Uncle Frank and Scott and Blake
I'm from the excessive hugging and surfing
From "Love others how you would want to be loved" and
My never-ending love for God, my Savior Jesus Christ who died on the cross for our sins
 I'm from Tennessee to Australia and Scotland,
I'm from fish tacos and virgin strawberry daiquiris
From the cousin who didn't see me in the street with his bike and ran me over like I was the pavement
From The Great Smoky Mountain National Park
I am from the beach and the country where I lived
Two different worlds, but my family made me one

Six Word Motto

Michael

Succeeding, failing, winning, and losing. Life.

Kiera

I'm from cleats

From flowers in the fields and fish in the lake

I'm from the brick house that overlooks the mountains, beautiful,
full of life

It sounds cheerful

I'm from evergreens and dogwoods

With cross shaped flowers

I'm from laughter and midnight mass

From Tom and Erin and Bailey

I'm from jokes and support

From "Rise and shine" and "Sleep tight"

I'm from the Catholic church with multi-colored stained glass
windows

I'm from Knoxville

Planta and pazzeles

From the mischief of Connor, protectiveness of Sean

I'm from many photo albums

From big family dinners, nice people, and the beauty of the
world

Six Word Motto

Dalton

Lost, get found. Blind, you will see.

Haley

I am from tissues

From Kleenex and Kimberly-Clark

I am from the dirt under the porch, musky and brown

It felt cool, like a refreshing glass of lemonade

I am from the daisies,

The bright yellow daisies

I'm from football games and sleeping after eating big meals

From Nicole and Kin and Kim

I'm from yelling when there are fumbles

From "Break a leg" and "Don't get in trouble, now"

I'm from Christianity

Praying every night before bed

I'm from Knoxville and Loudon County Fence Company

Chicken and apple pie

From the time my mom experienced a hurricane

The silliness of my brother

Memories stored in my hall closet

I am from a very fun-filled and adventurous life

Connor

I am from a fireplace with a blazing flame

From Case knives and Buick station wagons

I am from the place of wayward teenagers

Crazy, fast-paced

It felt like a place I could call home

I am from the mountain laurel

The shooting star

Different but beautiful

I'm from the Christmas mornings at Uncle Mike's and love of
the mountains

From my Dad Kevin and Uncle Jody and Ian

I'm from a strange sense of humor and being really cheap

From "Santa isn't real" and "It's good to be curious"

I'm from the flaming cross, House of God

I'm from Tennessee and the Cherokee

Deer and squirrel

From Dad's diving trip down in Nassau

And Ian's trip to Minnesota

I am from solving problems

Brian

I am from the country
From Ford and corn
I am from southern cooking
Loudness, family
I am from the trees, dirt, and mud of Tennessee
I'm from the Southwest and Apache Indians
From Thealoriabell and Efonda and Kera
I'm from the South
The Appalachian Mountains
From, "Never throw the first punch," and "Be respectful"
I'm from Christian and Native American beliefs
The Bible and nature
I'm from Maryville and Oklahoma
Indian tacos and country-fried steak and gravy
From the time my friend and I jumped off his roof
From all the family get-togethers for holidays
Crazy food fights
I'm from all the family pictures my grandmother puts on her
fridge
I am from the USA

Haiku

Brian

The dog barked all night
The dog kept the night awake
The night air was full

The cotton cloud cried
The moon stayed with it all night
It still cried all night

Michael

I am from taking the ball straight to the hoop

From Nike and Under Armour

I am from the back of the woods

Forest and lumber

It felt rough and bumpy

I am from the water

I'm like a rose

I need care and love to live

I'm from watching football

From Michael and Amanda and Brock

I'm from playing outside and brown eyes

From "An apple today keeps the doctor away" and

"Life is like a box of chocolates, you're never going to know

what you're going to get"

I'm from Baptists and belief that God is my creator

I'm from Auburndale, Florida, and Dutch ancestors

Cheese and sausage

From the basketball star in college and a hardworking mom

From pictures that hang on the walls

I am from being funny and kind

Six Word Memoir

Kat

Drawing will entertain me for hours.

Samuel

I am from PopTarts

From Toaster Strudels and Cheerios

From warm weather, it felt comfortable

I am from rose bushes, green with fragrant buds

From Ben and Nathan and Kelly

I'm from weird and amusing

From "Don't take candy from strangers" and "Be confident"

I'm from Christians, Baptists

From Knoxville

Turkey and mashed potatoes

From Ben at Easter

I'm from picture albums in the cabinet

I am from Maryville, Tennessee, the Volunteer State

Lauren

I am from pacifiers,

Chap Stick and pockets

I am from a strong brick foundation, strong coffee, and a great
family

It's incredibly safe and splendid

I am from the dandelions of the world, beautiful

I am from Tennessee football, fancy, and Amy

I'm from large eaters and clothes lovers

From "Hold my hand before you cross the road" and "Let's pray
before we eat"

 I'm from Maryville and good cooking

Coconut cream pies and small chocolates

From stories of licking all the chips and putting them back in the
bag

The meanness and kindness of Americans

I'm from above the rocky hills

I am from the athletic side of the world, the artsy kind of people,
and the shoe store

A Letter to Future Self

Nick

Dear future me (Nick),

I hope you have become a successful, kind, caring, and joyful person (even though I already know you have). If you still use letters as a form of messaging, (if not then there is no use in me sending this and it's probably just a waste of my time writing this which is going to make a difference in what I can succeed before you receive this so I should probably stop writing but I don't know any better so I am), then send me a letter back letting me know about what exactly I have become and how the world has changed.

Actually…the world may have blown up by now, so I could be writing to no one. Now that I think about it, I have no idea how I'll send this to you.

Sincerely,

A confused little you

Marley

I'm from shoes
From Nike and Saucony
I'm from the blue house
Rustic, peeling paint, it looked antique
I'm from the garden tulips, the ripe tomatoes, red and disgusting
I'm from the family game nights and extremely thick hair
From Mom and Dad and Henry
I'm from grilling on Friday nights and family dinners around the
table
From "Don't talk to strangers" and "Say 'Yes Ma'am' and 'Yes
Sir'"
I'm from church on Sunday, dressing nicely and looking clean
I'm from Tennessee, Ohio, and all over the world
Chicken and hot sauce
From the broken arm, and many shed tears
From "The Ball Game" on lazy days
From pictures in the shoebox on the fridge
I'm from love and hugs and "Goodbyes" and "Welcome backs"

Anonymous Author

I am from warm chocolate milk in the mornings
From Ovaltine and Maxwell House coffee
I am from the house next to the railroad tracks, white walls,
stained glass, metal swings
It roared at night when the train rumbled by, felt so peaceful
I am from the kudzu, green and thick, which still grows on the
fence nearby
The rose archway down the alley, soft red petals, long sharp
thorns
I'm from the all-day coffee drinking and slightly arching noses
From Kirks and Bains and Muellers
I'm from the quick tempers and killing kindness
From "Don't do stupid things" and "I love you. Be safe."
I'm from the Father, the Son, and the Holy Spirit
One Holy Catholic Apostolic church
I'm from New Mexico and Iowa
Tamales and sauerkraut
From working hard since a young age
And road trips taken in pick-up truck beds
From front yard and farmyard pictures
I am from crazy and sane, bitter and sweet
I am from all these things, and all these things I am

Sophia

I am from clocks

From Lysol and Apple

From the brick and siding-covered house

It is big and wide, it looks nice

I am from the rose and the tiger lily, bright and beautiful

I'm from cake and green eyes

From Claudia and James and Florence

I'm from the short and brown hair

From a pink floral dress and white shoes

I'm from Christianity and Catholicism

From New York and Germany

New York style pizza and pretzels

From the day my mom moved to New York City from Germany

From the shortness in my dad's family

I'm from family pictures in front of the Christmas tree

I am from New York and Tennessee

A Letter to My Past Self

Sophia

Dear 8th grade self,

I wish you would've known this, but since you don't I'm going to tell you. Eighth grade wasn't the best year in the beginning. There were some not very good times, but there were some really good times. Most of your friends will be there for you, and you'll be there for them, too. Don't freak out about anything, because what actually happened wasn't as bad as you thought it would be. There was a very good reason why it happened. I want you to know that you will figure it out soon enough. So, in the meantime, have fun. All the good things that happened and will happen to you will outweigh those few bad things. Everyone will come back together, and everyone will be healthy again. Don't assume things, and just remember that it'll all work out.

Sincerely,

Sophia

Alex

I am from China

From Nikon and Smith & Wesson

I am from crowded muggy places, busy, humid

It sounded like a bunch of bees

I am from the tree, the plant that is beautiful

I'm from the Christian and cancer

From Mom and Dad and Alex

I'm from the brave and smart

From the intelligent and stubborn

I'm from a Christian religion,

Belief that God is not dead

I'm from China

Noodles and candy

From the person who has helped me with a business

And from a photographer who is highly skilled

I'm from the Smoky Mountains

I am from the hill tops and the flat plains

Keiara

I am from whimsy, from true magical adoration that grows only
in rare places
And beautiful smiles with gold souls
I am from the warmth of my mother's arms, the feel of genuine
love
From the dinner table of my Papaw's and Granny's and
From dreaming of making it big
And being somewhere extraordinary and rare, a place where you
can find yourself
I am from the moons and the stars that bring me inner peace
I am from the monumental tree that used to swing me
A tree that often wore a nest of birds, at least that's what I swore
I am from the Christmas gatherings and the parading around in
Halloween costumes
From the sibling rivalries of Tamera and Jayden
Daughter of Tiffany and granddaughter of Myra
I'm from bright eyes and curly hair, from beautiful souls and
kind hearts
From "If you don't have anything nice to say, don't say anything
at all"
And "Don't forget to say 'please' and 'thank you'"
From praying and saying "God bless you "

Knowing God is always there even if nobody else is

I'm from the hospital of Saint Mary's

From fried chicken and biscuits and gravy

From Jayden's cutting his arm open skating

From running home to tell mom all about dance

I'm from beach family photo shoots, resulting in knee-deep
stacks of photo albums

I am from being myself and never letting anybody tell me
differently

I am from spreading positive vibes because life could be worse

From the foothills and the mountains

I am from Tennessee

Lindsey

"Trees"

The trees in the wind
Flowing side to side in the air
Oh, trees in the air

"Snow"

The snow is falling
The snowball rolls down the hill
Playing in the snow

Julia

I'm from lost remotes,
From Neosporin and Kleenex wipes
I'm from the big red brick house with the yellow dog in the front
yard
It feels like home
I'm from the dogwood trees and the flower pots in the backyard,
They look good when the flowers are alive
I'm from family movie nights and brown hair and eyes
From Brad and Christi and Jack
I'm from the family that forgets to shut the pantry door and
never turns off the lights
From "Brush your teeth" and "Throw away your trash"
I'm from New Providence Presbyterian Church, the one with the
big stones
I'm from Maryville
Steak and baked potatoes
From a mom who saved Jack from a snake and a dad who comes
to eat lunch with me at school
I'm from the family picture at Maryville College, when Andy
and Harrison wore jeans
I'm from competitive natures during games like "Apples to
Apples"

Hashtag Poem

Julia

#writea #poem #using #only #hashtags #she #said,

#make #a #baseball #card #she #said,

#get #your #parent #letter #signed #she #said,

#go #to #apps #w #she #said,

#go #to #BlackBoard #he #said,

#get #out #your #homework #and #a #red #or #green #pen #he #said,

#study #for #your #test #she #said,

#make #sure #and #be #in #your #seat #when #the #bell #rings #she #said,

#read #your #AR #book #he #said

Jay M

I am from McDonalds

From Little Debbies and Sour Patch Kids

I am from the small, outside, weird

It sounded peaceful

I am from the soft thorny rose and the white petal iris outside

your window

I'm from the praised and the small

From Mom and from Dad and shoe-stompers

I'm from the stubborn and the creative

From superstitions and horror tales

I'm from Christianity, the Heavenly Father's child

I'm from Bethlehem, bread and fish

From the stork that carried babies to and from

From the strong yet frail

The New Yorkers

I am from the heart and whatever it desires

Alex

I am from China

From Nikon and Smith and Weston

I am from the crowded and muggy places, busy, humid

It sounded like a bunch of bees

I am from the trees and plants, beautiful

I'm from Christians and cancer

From Mom and Dad and Alex

I'm from the brave and smart

From the intelligent and stubborn

I'm from a Christian religion,

Believing that God is not dead

I'm from China

Noodles and candy

From an intelligent person who helped me with a business

And photography

And the highly skilled

Now living in the Great Smoky Mountains

I am from the hill tops and the flat plains

Addison

I am from home
From Hershey's and Coca-Cola
I'm from the white home on the circle with a big pear tree in the
yard
The pears are sour
I am from the bush in the back, the big purple, fragrant one
And meeting at Grandma's house for Christmas Eve
From Pete and Kathy, From Dick and Gerry, Steve and Wendy
From, "You're going to break your neck" and
"Don't sit that close to the TV," and "Finish your food before
dessert"
From "Jesus loves me" and Sunday sermons
From my great-grandfather's farm
From my grandfather's love for the Tennessee Volunteers
From family photos for Christmas cards
I am from that one white house on Martin Street
I'm from Maryville, Tennessee

Jasmyne

I am from books

From Barnes & Noble and Hastings

I am from the lightning bugs in the front yard

Beautiful, bright and flying with energy

A moving string of Christmas lights

I am from dogwoods and peonies

Bright, colorful, and beautiful

I am from trips to Cades Cove riding around the loop

I am from the impatience from Nana, Papaw, and Mom

I'm from helping with dinner and watching football

From "Always be yourself" and "Always respect yourself and others"

I'm from going to church on Sunday and believing in Jesus

From Blount Memorial Hospital

Baked beans and ribs

From Nana thinking a water bottle was a jelly fish and the craziness of my cousins

I am from the mountains where all the pictures were taken

I am from a small town in Tennessee with lots of books and lots of love

Memorable Moment

Jasmyne

It was the day before I was supposed to leave for Utah to visit my cousins. I was in the car with my mom on the way to the store. We were going down a hill and had the music up loud and were singing and dancing. We didn't have a stop sign, so we kept going but the person to the left of us ran his stop sign and was nearly a foot away from our car. My mom was paying attention and swerved to the right and barely missed the car. This was a memorable moment for me because it shows just how fast life can be taken away. No matter where you are or what you're doing, you could die at any moment. It taught me not to take life for granted and to always do more good than bad. You never know when the end of your life is coming and you want to be known for the good you've done.

Zach

I am from earbuds
From Skullcandy and Beats
I am from the bricks, solid and red, cold and rough
I am from the trees
The oaks, tall and sturdy
I am from summer picnics and brown eyes
From Steve, Shannon and Joanne
I am from lazy Sundays and busy weeks
"Treat everyone with respect" and "Pick up after yourself"
I am from Fort Meyers, Florida and Buffalo, New York
From Pierogi and pickles
From my dad deep sea diving
And my grandfather working on computers
All this in photos, stored away in the closet
I am from the music generation
Motivated and determined

Ellie

I am from lollipops and gummy bears
From "That's So Raven" and "hide-and-seek"
From good 'ole East Tennessee
Magnificent, surreal, it feels of the moist air from the mountains
I am from clover in the backyard and pollen in the air
I am from car rides up to the mountains, loud and annoying
I am from Nana and Pop, Mom and Dad
I am from loudly singing in the car and listening to music
From "Nightmares aren't real" and "Eat your vegetables"
I am from church on Sundays and beautiful stained glass
windows
I am from Maryville, the place where I've been all my life, full
of yummy BBQ and potato salad
From mom telling me, every time we pass "that" building, that
my great-grandfather built it
And my dad taking me to breakfast in the morning on weekends
I am from a family who takes lots of pictures and when they are
finished they take some more
I am from family and friends who love me unconditionally
I can never thank them enough

Letter to Future Self

Ellie

Dear Ellie,

This is 14-year-old Ellie in her freshman year of high school. Everything is going well, and fall break is almost here! I am writing this so future Ellie can read this later on when you are far out of high school and see if you have accomplished any of the goals 14-year-old Ellie has set for you. I am hoping that this will brighten your day and bring back memories from earlier in your life that will make you smile.

I hope you have graduated Maryville High School with a great GPA, and succeeded at many things. I think about my future quite often, so I hope it's been great so far! You have many years ahead of you so make every day count. Enjoy your life. Don't waste it with people that don't make you happy, don't make you cry from laughing so hard, or people that try to change who you are. Enjoy your freedom that hopefully you have reached. I hope that you have your driver's license and are being safe and making good decisions. I dream about going to a wonderful college and meeting wonderful people and leading myself to a wonderful life! Education is very important, and I hope that you have taken your high school years seriously and have paved yourself a great road to a successful life. You have lost many friends and gained many friends. I hope that your dedication to being happy and dedication to God has not loosened but only tightened and grown. I pray that you haven't let peer pressure get the best of you, and you have stayed true to who you are. Don't let guys change your identity and make you have tunnel vision. Let things go and move on. Take moments to yourself and just breathe. Close your eyes and relax. Don't get too stressed over little things. I hope you have grown out of procrastination. I hope you are a mature woman who can stand up for yourself and what you believe in. You only get one life to live.

I hope it has been great so far. Enjoy being around people who make you happy. Laugh so hard you cry. Love the people around you. Give back to the people that have given you everything. Accomplish great things. Follow your heart. Live your dreams. Enjoy life. You only get one.

Love,
14 year-old Ellie

Mason

I am from baseballs

From Nike and Adidas

I am from the valley, green and low

It tasted sweet

I am from trees

And the rocky hillside

I'm from Georgia football

From Alex and Amy and Colby

I'm from baseball weekends and football Fridays

From "Mind your manners" and "Respect your elders"

I'm from reading the Bible and giving thanks

I'm from Knoxville,

Chicken and beans

From riding my grandfather's tractor in the grassy field

And leaving my grandma's house with my belly full

From pictures in a shoebox

I am from my family, religion, and sports

Six Word Memoir

Mason

God, family, baseball: the three priorities.

Raina

I am from Barbie

From dolls and playhouses

I am from the yellow house on top of the hill

Inviting, friendly

It sounds like chaos and happiness

I am from dogwood trees by the patio

And gardens in the woods

I'm from hide 'n go seek by the Christmas tree and green eyes

From Maeleah and Lairame and Daelyn

I'm from giving one another nicknames

From loud singing and dancing in the kitchen

From "Please" and "Thank you"

And "Put others first"

I'm from praying before every meal

And church on Sundays

I'm from my Great Aunt Nell's apple pie and Grandmama's

fried green tomatoes

Cherokee and Belgian roots

From the time we moved to Oklahoma, to moving home again

And the curly hair I get from Poppa Don

I'm from pictures hanging everywhere they can fit

I am from my family, the most spectacular people I know

Haiku

Raina

Kittens leapt softly
Through the grass they sweetly went
Leaping kittens play

Swinging on the porch
With Grandmama by my side
Listening to rain

Tiara

I am from Chick-fil-a
From Apple and Microsoft Windows
I am from the house on the corner
With medium-sized lots full of cars
It looked average
I am from roses, pretty and pink
I'm from sit down dinners and social time
From William and Elizabeth and David
I'm from lovable, sometimes sweet
From "Be happy" and "Not to worry"
I'm from a Presbyterian Church
Where everyone is a child of God
Quesadillas and enchiladas
Adopted by Crystal and William (he's the best)
I am from Puerto Rico, ancestors on my mom's side
And Ireland, ancestors from my biological dad
I'm from East Tennessee

A.R.

I am from books

From Lay's potato chips and circus peanuts

I am from a little town in the backwoods of West Virginia

It smelled like cow manure

I am from mountains and dandelion bouquets my sister and I
used to pick for my mom

I am from family get-togethers and card games

From Memama, Debra Greer, and Kimberly Reynolds Carpenter

I am from Christ's followers and big meals

From "Don't plop down on that couch!" and "I love you"

I am from John 3:16 and listening to K-Love every time we get
in the car

From "He leadeth me beside still waters"

I am from North and South

Green beans and macaroni 'n cheese

From the legend of my Granddaddy Frank and his hatred for
anything other than butt cheeks on his couch to the fingers my
Uncle Howard cut off of my Uncle Gary

From shelves and shoe boxes of family photos, bursting full and
begging to be opened to reveal once again all of the fond
memories they contain

I am from "The apple doesn't fall far from the tree" and "You
look just like your mama"

"A Woman is like a Rose" by A.R.

A girl is like a rose
just a small bud at first,
innocent and helpless,
but with the potential to
bloom into a gorgeous young lady,
WITH THE RIGHT CARE

A young lady is like a rose
still tender and dainty.
However, she is not so helpless anymore.
A she is more exposed to the world,
she develops thorns to protect her
from the evil of the World.
Thorns of Love, Faith, Kindness, even fear.
If she is well gardened with roots in the good soil of the Holy
Spirit,
she will flourish.
But if she is planted in dirt of the world,
she will shrivel and die.
A young lady will burst into a woman,
IF SHE IS PURSUED BY THE RIGHT CARETAKERS.

A woman is like a rose,
with a bloom of purity, grace and beauty.
Her petals are a price well earned,
from striving to grow towards the Son
And push past the weeds that are the devils temptations.
Although she has thorns, she is still a wonderful creation.
Those who have gloves of Compassion
may touch this flower.
BUT THOSE WHO DO NOT, WILL DRAW AWAY.

Park

I am from trees

From Heinz and Intel

I am from the red brick porch

Hot on a summer day, crimson in the sunlight

It felt rough and hot

I am from the dogwood

And the lake, blue and peaceful

I'm from Christmas dinner and a sense of humor

From June and Carol and Roy

I'm from easy to get along with

From "Do unto others as you would have others do unto you"

and "If you want respect, you give respect"

I'm from Christianity

From Tampa, Florida

Tomatoes and pickles

From Great Grandmother who rode a jet ski for her 90th birthday

and the police officer

With the pictures in the living room

I am from all of the nature around me

Haiku

Vishwa

The bunny ran home
Across the plains to a well
Running quietly

The rain dripped calmly
Down the street into the lake
Pitter pattering

Sydney

I'm from Blount Memorial Hospital, where my mom worked
An amazing place
From high school volleyball and Big Zax's Snack Meals
I'm from a big green house with a porch swing in a
neighborhood with lots of people
From buttercups and bright colors like yellow and orange
I'm from tech class with Mrs. McCall
She is awesome
From a cruise that went to Mexico and the Cayman Islands
I'm from friends and camping and Tennessee Volunteer football
I'm from a family of five, with lots of extended family
And a blessed home
From California rolls and Nerd slushes from Sonic
From fluffy poodles
I'm from church, a pastor's daughter, a Christian family
A rebel from Maryville Junior High School
I'm from places just like you
But from the Kenny, Anita, Hannah, and Mckenzie all my own

Found Poem

Sydney

School ain't fun, but,

To do our best; we must do what is required.

School matters.

So don't give up.

Gavin

I am from a bed

Cool sheets and fluffy pillows

From the rusty metal chair in front, old and tired

I am from oak trees and the red bushes, both beautiful and wild

From Christmas dinner and love

From Jason and Pier and the great Shannon

I am from judgmental but caring

From monsters under the bed

And monsters in the closet

I am from the United States of America

Burgers and pizza

From blonde hair and brown eyes

I am from where I am from, and no one can take that away

Benjamin

I am from cookies

From PopTarts and Kentucky Fried Chicken

I am from a two-story brick building, red and bland

It looked boring

I am from cactus and the tree

Small, green and spikey

I'm from buying ornaments at Christmas and wearing glasses

From Kim and Todd and Jerry

I'm from yelling and trying the best you can

From "Don't play in the road" and "Don't touch that"

I'm from Jesus and the all-loving God

I'm from Chattanooga

Bratwurst and soda bread

From the time we moved closer to family and Grandfather

helped us

The love from my sister

Somewhere over the rainbow

I am from the general kindness from my heart and staying by my

friends' sides

Brittany

I am from pizza

From Diet Coke and Milky Way bars

I'm from the brick house with a big yard, an old swing set and a
wooden fence

It smelled like freshly cut grass and Ravioli casserole

I am from the iris of Tennessee and the cherry tree, pink and
pretty

I am from Christmas on Christmas Eve and red hair

From Melissa and Dusty

I am from our horrible tempers and aggravation of each other

From "I love you" and "Cause I said so"

I am from church and Jesus

I am from Maryville, Tennessee

From glasses

I am from blue eyes and red hair

Esther

I am from laundry basket
From warm vanilla sugar lotion and Paris Amour perfume
I am from the giant house with a playground in the back
Faded, antique, it tasted like chocolate
I am from massive magnolia trees and pointy gumballs, whose
hurtful spikes I remember as they fell to the ground
I'm from chocolate chip cookies and Christmas Eve crackers
From Tracy and Jack
I'm from non-singers and non- dancers
From "Don't throw the ball in the house" and "Be aggressive!"
I'm from rocked out worship and praise, from Faith Promise
I'm from Maryville, Tennessee
Corn and pumpkin pie
I'm from the three teeth my brother lost and the skull my brother
fractured
I'm from family pictures taken in Grandma's front yard
Framed by huge blooming flowers and several orange fish in the
pond
I am from sweet moments with my family
I cherish them every day

Allison

I am from the valleys of Tennessee

From volleyball and warm southern days

I am from the small house on a cul-de-sac, quiet and homey

It feels like a warm Tennessee memory

I am from lily-of-the-valley, dogwoods and oak trees, pretty and fragrant

I'm from football games and days on the river

I'm from laughter

From Robert and Sharon, the sister of Adam

I'm from endless baseball games and warm summer days at the pool

From sleeping in while having fun with my friend

From "Jesus Loves Me" and "Be anything you want to be"

I'm from church every Sunday and nightly devotions

I'm from Maryville, Tennessee

Chicken and banana pudding

From the stories of my family

And the love and grace of Grandmother Earley

I am from a Jesus-loving, grace-giving, southern-living family

Madeline

I am from chicken feed
From shovels and buckets
I am from the red brick barn
Looking pretty big on our little farm
I'm from basil, thyme, and lavender
The smell's so clean and fresh
I'm from the eating on the couch
And really long legs
From Jimmy and Denise and Tom
I'm from cooking all day and sleeping all night
From "Never let someone tell you what to do" and "God made
you perfect"
I'm from God can help you through anything, no matter how
hard it is
From the Mom's in the hospital again
And her long brown hair sprawled out as she sleeps on her little
couch
I'm from a Marine Corps haircut and the gun tucked in his jeans
I am from long, dark brown hair and being the tallest in my
family
On that little secret farm

Tommy

I am from basketballs

From Spalding and Wilson

I am from cracks on the porch steps

Creepy, scary, it feels slimy

I am from trees, the tall oak, so green and beautiful

I'm from Sunday dinners and Wednesday breakfasts

From "Be the best you can be" and "Never give up"

I'm from Christianity and going to Heaven

I'm from a Tennessee hospital

Rolls and Hamburgers

From the brown hair of my mother

And the toughness of my uncle

From the photographs in the cabinet at my aunt's house

I am from Tennessee, I am a Smith

Haiku
Jared and Nick

An old silent pond
A frog jumps into the pond
Splash! Silence again

Autumn moonlight
A worm digs silently
Into the chesnut

Abby

I am from Arizona

From Cold Stone Creamery and Diamondback games

I am from brick walls and the sandy ground

It looks amazing and wonderful

I am from the cactus, the heat, and the Saguaro Cactus Blossom

I'm from the brown-eyed and brown-haired

From Christine and Mark and Austin

I'm from laughing loud and standing tall

From the Tooth Fairy and Santa Claus

I'm from a Baptist Church with awesome preachers

I'm from Scottsdale Arizona

Trout and corn and squash

From the always talking aunts to the storytelling grandfather

Kept in a photo album in the attic

I am from basketball playing and baseball games

From the hot and sunny Scottsdale, Arizona

Bailey

I am from long walks down my grandmother's road
From Crayola and Play-Doh
I'm from club houses made out of sheets
Dim and warm
It felt careless and free
I am from maple trees to climb on and honeysuckle, the
fragrance sweet and warm
I'm from Sunday school mornings and light brown hair
From Cristy and Trent and Mamaw
I am from goodnight prayers, camping and 4th of July fireworks
From "Get your socks back on!"
And "Don't change for anyone but yourself"
I'm from cross necklaces and Noah's Ark stickers
I'm from Vonore
Buffalo hamburgers and fried chicken
From the dog I once had and named Stormy
The music on my mom's car radio
I'm from the family pictures on the fireplace
From the Red Hot Chili Peppers
And trying to find who I am

Harrison

I am from baseball

From A1 Steak Sauce and Tombstone Pizza

I am from a hill in southern Illinois, quiet

It was beautiful

I am from dandelions and daisies

It was simple

I'm from wild Christmas parties and German heritage

From Pat and Dave and Duck

I'm from funny jokes and euchre

From "Go to college" and "I love you"

I'm from the cross and Jesus

I'm from Mascoutah and Germany

Bratwurst and Marzipan

I'm from my Grandpa Harry who owned a lumber yard and
worked his whole life

From my father, who did the same

I'm from a big white house and all my memories

I am from southern Illinois

Proud of being born and raised in Mascoutah and Albers

Hunter

I am from computers

From Xbox and flash drives

I am from the mountains

Raccoons, trees

It felt relaxing

I am from dirt

Poison ivy

Allergic reactions

I'm from graduation parties and a sense of humor

From Jay and Renee and Landon

I'm from long road trips and eating dinner together

From "Santa isn't real" and "Eat your vegetables"

I'm from church, Catholic

From Knoxville and Germany

Hamburgers and hot dogs

From Dad walking to the ranger station when the car broke down

And crazy Landon

From Crater Lake

I am from the mountains, the only home for me

Patience

I am from Knoxville, Tennessee
From the Volunteers and Marble City
I am from the loud, busy streets of the city
Sad, dark, and noisy
I am from the mountains of the Rockies
Where the soil is rough
And I'm from the unlucky where family traditions are a bore
I am from the Presleys, Couches, and Russells
Where the sign of love is to wrestle and to take care of one
another for there is nothing better
From "All we have is each other" and "You should get along
with one another"
I'm from The Church of Jesus Christ of Latter Day Saints
Where caffeine is something our bodies should not absorb
I'm from Europe and America
From corn and tobacco
I'm from the patience my mom knew she would need with me
From brothers Blaze and Kane (born August 25, 2003 and died
September 27, 2003)
Kane was set free and my mother was grief-stricken for a while
I'm from Cades Cove where the ground was fertile, the place
mom loves so dearly that we go there every year
I am from Marble City, where the grass barely shows

A.Z.

I am from war movies

Diapers and forests

From the creek so cold it tasted like plants and dirt

I am from sunflowers, bright and happy

I am from meat and sports

From Azure, Elizah, Adrian and Bruce

I'm from family that love baseball and men who served in the
military

From having stories read to me

I'm from hiking and camping in the Great Smoky Mountains

From "You will to grow up to be a strong and beautiful girl" and
"You will look up to your brother when you get older"

I'm from a Christian family

From Naples Florida

I'm from a grandfather who has lived through more than three
presidents

Pumpkin pies and noodles

I'm from Grandfather in the war a long time ago and my real
father having sixty-nine percent disability

Family pictures located at my grandmother's house in a trunk by
her bed

I am a strong and beautiful girl from Naples, Florida, and
Maryville, Tennessee

Hope

I'm from a place where love hurts

Where the dirt is mushy and country girls go wild

I'm from a place in a little town that's not so big

From drama and bumps in the road, but family love no matter
what

I'm from a place where "If you're so kindly rude to my ma or pa,
I will lay a hand on you"

From a place with a lot of lakes

I'm from a place that others call a town tiny, but I call it mighty
and home

From a place where my friends never forget me even, when I
leave for they know I will always come back

I'm from a place where feelings matter, where we know the right
things to do

From a place with southern accents and country voices

From a place where you can get to know me and decide on your
own if you want to be a part of my bumpy journey

From scrapes and bruises, but at the end of the day a place I
know as home

Halie

I am from Justin boots
Durango's and Maurice's
I am from the Great Smoky Mountains, beautiful and airy
It looks breathtaking
I am from dogwoods and irises
From good home cooked meals and southern accents
From Kelley and Jeff and Dorothy
I'm from loving, caring, and kindness, with a touch of southern
charm
From "Be strong and brave"
I'm from Jesus' hands and His love
From Scots-Irish and Cherokee
Fried chicken and sweet tea
I'm from Maryville, Tennessee
I'm from the way grandmother and papaw met
From where my great-uncle played corn cob jail
I'm from the love of my mother
From pictures of my great uncles, aunts, and great-grandparents
I am from country music, cowboy boots, floral dresses, and
singing in the choir on Sunday

Emilee

I am from love
From Lip Smackers and Hubba Bubba gum
I am from The Great Smoky Mountains, humid and beautiful
It looks amazing
I'm from roses and the sea, beautiful and sharp
I am from good home cooking and blue eyes
From short tempers and kindness
I'm from "You are amazing" and "You can do anything you set
your mind to"
I am from Jesus' love, a Christian
From Maryville, Tennessee
Fried chicken and cornbread
I'm from the brain tumor my mom had when I was seven
From her making it through and having no cancer
I'm from three surgeries of my grandfather who was attacked by
dogs
I'm from the pictures under my mom's bed
I am an easygoing country girl with lots of goals, and lots of
people to see me succeed

Letter to Future Self

Emilee

Hello Emilee,

You are now 21 years old. I hope you have gotten into the forensic science academy. I hope you graduated high school with a 3.0 GPA or higher. Remember how you loved friends Taylor, Jasmine, and Halie? I hope you have found bliss in life. I assume you have had your first heartbreak, if not you are really behind everybody else. I imagine you have had a couple of drinks. I also think you are probably doing well in college. Is it everything you thought it would be at 14? I hope you still want to be a forensic scientist. You have been dreaming about it since sixth grade. You loved watching "Bones" and "CSI" and "NCIS." Real life forensic science probably totally different than on TV. I mean it has to be, you are solving actual crimes. I believe that you will do really well in life and I am glad you still have hopes and dreams. You will be alright; you are strong. Just believe you can do it and you will do it.

Love
Your 14 year old self

Caitlin

I'm from catching fireflies with siblings on late summer nights
From Mason jars filled to the rim with Louisiana sweet tea
From a loud chaotic home filled with friends and relatives
From the pool in the backyard, cool and refreshing
I'm from family with hearts bigger than bank accounts
From early Sunday mornings at East Maryville Baptist Church
I am from burned Ramen noodles and weekly homemade tacos
From Sunday family get-togethers and classic jokes from Papaw
I'm from girl's day with my Nana and sisters when we go to the
movies and shop
From walls filled with photographs representing great memories
I am from two puppies filling the air with loud barks and
squeaks
I'm from home

Rebecca

I am from Ralph Lauren perfume
American flags and fishing poles
I am from the humid sunrise in Texas
Warm and light, it looked like gold rays I imagine are in Heaven
I am from palm trees and dogwoods, alive and beautiful
I'm from long drives and laughter
From Beau and Dad and Mom
I'm from leadership and compassion
From "Always try your best!" and "You could've done better"
I'm from undecided spirits, careless and free
From Jacksonville and local farms
Pear preserves and artichokes
From the way my grandparents travel the country
The pride Dad radiated as he stood in his uniform
The totes upon totes of pictures stacked in the closet
I am from seeing new things, from California to Florida
With memories being made

Bryson

I am from playin' cards
From Coca-Cola and burgers
I am from the valley, cool and calm
It feels like home as soon as you step foot on the land
I am from the trees and the mountains, with leaves that turn
crimson in the fall
I'm from homemade ice cream and family time
From Larry and Linda and Ken
I'm from jokers and laughers
From "Treat others the way you want to be treated" and "Don't
fight, ya'll"
I'm from Christ who saves me and God His Father
I'm from Maryville
Mashed potatoes and steak n' gravy
From the old guy who climbs the telephone poles and the
grandfather who retired from the supply company
From a box full of scrapbooks filled with pictures of the past
I am from my crazy and loving family

Haiku
Mason

A cherry blossom

Lifted upon the breeze

Flutters to the ground

Dancing flames of death

A scar against the green forest

The forest burns to ashes

Dalton

I am from the foothills of the Smokies
From corn eatin' and sweet tea drinkin'
I am from mountains, fragile and majestic
Felt like there is no place I'd rather be
I am from trees, a rough skeleton with a coat of green
I'm from the river and brown hair
From Greg and Heather and Owen
I'm from fire and swallowing leaves below
From "Rocky Top" and "Jesus Loves Me"
I am from the cross where Jesus Christ died for me
I'm from Maryville
Barbecue and steak
From the time my uncle put his life on the line in a building on
9/11
I am from Maryville, Tennessee living in Ol' Rocky Top

Elizabeth

I am from music
From romantic novels and cream sodas
I am from a southern, joyful family
Lively and boisterous
It sounds like a marching band tune, and cheers of my kin as the
soccer player scores
I am from irises and prickly roses
From the old house in the middle of the street
Brick-like and scarlet colored
It felt like home when I looked in my front yard and saw flowers
and my brother's soccer goal
I am from rhododendrons and cherry trees, with their juicy,
crimson cherries, ripe in the spring
I'm from large Christmas Eve gatherings with family and many
cousins
From Melissa and Andy and Alex
I'm from loud family gatherings and arguments over who gets to
clean up the Christmas tree needles
From a saxophone-playing grandfather who passed away before
we could meet and the niece of the famous Wright children
From Pilot Club swimmers
I am from tunes from a clarinet
I'm from Catholics of Sunday masses, and Christian music

I'm from Tennessee and Ancestral Germany

Marzipan and Haribo Gold gummy bears

I'm from Ursula, my immigrant grandmother from Germany

And the native Grammy named Jewel from Elizabethton,

Tennessee

Nathan

I am from prunes

From Legos and Sony

I am from the long forgotten layout of the rooms downstairs

Cold, old, it seemed very bright

I am from bamboo, the gingko

The sight which I still see

I am from fruit salad and deep voices

From Glen, and Megan, and Evan

I'm from stubbornness and music

From "Suck it in" and "Stand up straight"

I'm from monthly lunches, with people as good as the food

I'm from Washington D.C. and wooden shoes

Oliebollen and waffles

From the skull fracture after falling from the second floor

From Disney trips I didn't go on

Photographs in the middle, medium shelf downstairs, chock with

forgotten gold and embarrassing moments

I'm from somewhere in there, the last one, for now, of course

Parker

I am from hand-me-downs

From blue jeans and Wrangler

I'm from the towering home on the hill

The powerful, majestic home

It looked like a citadel

I am from dogwood trees and sunflowers, bright and strong

From the hard work of construction and the gift of an author

From Hennery Hill, Todd and Lorrie Zeiger

I'm from stubbornness and courage

From "Pray to the Lord for strength" and "Pray about all things"

I'm from Christianity, and the belief that one day I will see loved

ones again in Heaven

From Knoxville and the Irish

Potatoes and chips

I'm from courage and bravery in the line of duty

From the strength of a mom who kept my world from falling

apart

The dusty book on the shelf

I am from a strong family of hard workers who love and respect

the man I am becoming

Six Word Memoir

Parker

Started from the bottom now here.

Olivia

I am from books

From Mac computers and swimming pools

I am from silly, crazy, fun

It looks like a carnival

I am from mountains and green trees

I'm from Christmas dinners and Friday night movies

From Clint and Mellissa and Bella

I'm from pranksters and magicians

From "Don't play with your food" and "Be nice"

I'm from Christianity, the Church

I'm from America

Apple pie and fried chicken

From the time I first beat my wonderful dad in Mario cart

The perfect chaos of three little cousins

The backyard

I am from the craftsy, artsy, and interesting

Jonah

I'm from a house
From Crayola and Fisher Price
I'm from a brick house
Red and grayish
It sounded like cars passing by on the road
The dogwood trees
Brown bark with green leaves
I'm from Sunday lunches and Saturday suppers
From David and Susan and Coy
I'm from the loud and the talkative
From "I'm not sleeping, I'm resting my eyes" and "Don't pull
the dogs tail"
I'm from *In Christ Alone*, saved by faith
I'm from the Volunteer state
Corn bread and biscuits and gravy
From the war my grandfather was in and the music my brother
makes
In the hallway on the left side
I'm from Maryville, Tennessee

Six Word Memoir

Kaitlyn

Ninth grade's harder than you think.

Parker

I'm from Twinkies

From "I Can't Believe It's Not Butter" and Scuf

I'm from Blount Memorial Hospital

It looked sanitary

I'm from the sausage tree

I'm from sleep

From Michelle and Parker and Jim

I'm from food, eating, and sleeping

From "You look like your mom" and "If you eat too much

candy, your teeth will fall out"

I'm from Blount Memorial Hospital

Sugar Babies and Skittles

I'm from Maryville, Tennessee

Friendly

Bailey

I am from bobby pins

From Sketchers and Crayola

I am from the playroom

Open, cold

It felt like the Arctic

I am from the pine tree, standing tall like a giant over me

I'm from the Maryville Intermediate School gym

And dark skin

From Tim and Marie

I'm from "Gotcha!" and "Reeeeefreshing!"

From "Don't bow down to idols" and "Do not lie"

I'm from Jesus dying on the cross,

And "Jesus loves me, this I know"

I'm from Maryville

Lumpia and hash brown casserole

From my dad's finger falling off and his breaking his nose twice

On the stairwell with one light are many fun memories

I am second... and I am saucy

Ciera

I am from Dial soap and electronics
From Samsung and Apple
I'm from the grass in my yard
Green, full
It tastes like dirt
I am from roses with green leaves and branches
I'm from babies and love
From Christie and Patrick and Aubri and John
I'm from the weirdness and loudness of my siblings
From "Use common sense" and "I love you"
I'm from Christianity and loving God
I'm from Florida with my parents
Pasta and strudel from Italy and Germany
From the death of my grandmother and the love of my parents
I'm from pictures in the picture frame, hanging on my wall, in
my dining room with the others
I am a crazy person from Florida
I am me

Haiku

Ciera

The leaves are falling

The trees is losing its leaves

Fall is on its way

School is in session

The students roam the hallways

Summer is now gone

Taylor

I'm from bicycles
From Razor scooters and Converse shoes
I'm from the old brown house with the shiny red door in the
middle of the street
Rustic and ancient
It sounded like animals hopping and skipping in the forest
The trees were bright with fall all year 'round
I'm from huge Thanksgiving meals and bright blonde hair
From Chris and Nancy and Debra
I'm from the ability to talk for hours
And sweetness sweeter than honey
From "Everything will be alright" and "It's okay to make
mistakes"
I'm from the love of the Lord and Savior, Jesus Christ
And Bible readings with my family
I'm from the beautiful state of Tennessee
Sweet Irish cream and the taste of Indian corn
From the time my dad had shoulder surgery
And the time when my mom brought home my new puppy
I'm from a large album containing an abundance of shared
family memories and stories
I'm from Maryville, Tennessee, a place where people are
friendly, and flowers seem to always grow

Noah

I'm from swing sets

From Scentsy and Pampered Chef

I'm from the home that always had people over, clean, loud

It smelled like something was always cooking

I'm from tall trees, the cacti, green and rough

I'm from Thanksgiving dinner and loud relatives

From Emily and Jenny and Sarah

I'm from watching TV and eating dinner

From going to the park on Sundays

From "Treat people how you want to be treated" and "Be quiet if
you want to go play."

I'm from Jesus is our Savior and everyone has a place in Heaven

I'm from Arizona and Nashville

Beans and mashed potatoes

I'm from playing in the dark with my loud cousins

The times my brother had to go to the hospital because of the
bugs

The pictures on the side wall of the stairs

I'm from the cool fall nights when the leaves fall

Sammi

I am from dance
From Bloch and Capezio
I am from the stage
Hot and bright, it smells like sweat
I am from the waltz of the flowers
The waltz, so fluid and smooth
I'm from prayers backstage and huge smiles
From Clara and Cinderella and Don Q
I'm from cheesy smiles
That I, too, have done too many times
From first position and fifth
I'm from different people from different places
I'm from backstage, fake eyelashes and snacks
From the story of the Nutcracker, with Clara, the young girl
With many pictures and memories
I am from the stage
Because I am a dancer

Jacob

I'm from a house

From Microsoft Windows and Linux

I'm from the house in a small suburban neighborhood

It looked like a stereotypical community

I'm from the maple tree, the tree whose leaf stood as our flag

I'm from the yearly trips to my homeland and honor

From Jennifer and Jim

I'm from hard workers, always persistent

From "I told you so" and "Help me with this"

I'm from skepticism and open minds

I'm from Calgary and Jim's sailboat

Seafood and well-cooked food

From the house my father built

And the car we are building together

From Calgary and Maryville

I'm from the busy city and the quiet suburbs

Emma

I am from light bulbs

From LED and Halogen

I am from a stable home

Strong and secure

It felt complete

I am from the Fire Lily, the German Alps

I am from the angel biscuit

And dark skin, which is always present

From Millsaps and Hettmansberger and Lanes

I'm from the big jerks and the educators

From "Always brush your teeth" and "It takes two to tango"

I'm from "God bless the little children" and "Hard work pays off"

I'm from Germany and Brazil and Wurst

From the times I played soccer with Erin

And the soup can in my pillow

From memories stored inside my grandmother's cabinet

I am from the hard-working family who strives to be better every new day

Six Word Memoir

Emma

I cannot wait for the weekend!

Maria

I am from airline food
From Lufthansa and unknown faces
I am from the homegrown fruit
Smiles and memories
It tasted like before, when we were little
I am from the sun and the wild poppies, periodically picked up
by our family on walks
I'm from singing Christmas carols at the top of my lungs and
competitiveness
From Aunt Patty and Sean and Kostanza
I'm from arguing over board game rules and the dread of chores
From "Be careful little eyes what you see" and "Don't go out by
yourself at night"
I'm from mission trips, gospel singing groups, and Bible studies
I'm from small Greek villages and Florida Gators,
Goat cheese and greasy gyros
From the disobedience resulting in an "I told you so"
And seven stitches
From the sad move to another place
I am from dusty pictures in old summer villas
I am from long hours at the beach and European summers with
my family

Tommy

I am from football

From Gamecocks and the South Eastern Conference

I am from the middle class house

White, decent size

Though it appears small

I am from the tree, the maple, big with many leaves

I am from visits to my grandparents on Sunday and dark hair

From Tad and Christy and Kelly

I am from cooking and watching sports

From "Respect your elders" and "Do your best"

I am from a Christian, loving family

I am from Charleston, South Carolina

Shrimp and flounder

From the Gamecock football games with my dad and granddad,

who was a Commodore in the Navy

I'm from pictures on the walls in the hall

I am from South Carolina and respect

Emmie

I am from stars in the sky
From Nike and Mayfield
I am from the garden
Green, lively, like a jungle
I am from cherry trees and pear trees, with no fruit
I'm from names spanning generation to generation and smart
minds
From Brayden and Leyton and Camden
I'm from artists and humor
From a best friend's death and the gain of a new pet
I'm from *The Book of Mormon a*nd Latter Day prophets
I'm from Texas and across the seas
Rice and corn
From the time my brother broke his knee
And pictures on the walls
I am from the craziest and the strangest, the ones I love best

Victoria

I am from books

From *Harry Potter* and *Series of Unfortunate Events*

I am from the living room

Warm, comforting

It felt soothing

I am from vases of flowers on the dining room table

Vibrant coloration

I'm from homemade cooking and dark hair

From Janet Cabe-Inman and Brian Inman and Jessie Cabe

I'm from goofiness and strong country accents

From being spoiled rotten and being a goofball

I'm from Christianity; I am a child of the one true King

I'm from Maryville, Tennessee

Pumpkin pie and home-grown vegetables

From sitting around the camp fire beside my mom and laughing

at stories told by my grandma

I am from Maryville, Tennessee, loved by God and family

I am a lover of books, cooking, baking, and sports

Sam

I am from grass

From Clorox and Gap

I am from the house of adventure

Fun, warm, familiar, it tasted sweet

I am from water, flowing with new rains

From Beth and Jason and Walt

I'm from creators and doers

From Santa and the Tooth Fairy

I'm from church with art on Sundays

I'm from East Tennessee

Apple pie and eggs

From the small feet in the living room

From when I was young and the trees were full of adventure

Madison

I am from chocolate chip cookies
From Tollhouse and McCormick
I am from the swing on the patio
Filled with memories and fun times, near and dear to my heart
It felt so fun to feel the thrill of flying
I am from trees and flowers that filled the backyard
Colorful, beautiful, and sweet-smelling
I'm from the love of cheese and brown hair
From Ralph and Tammie and Mattie Louise
I'm from hikes on Sundays and crazy family dinners
I'm from "Shut Up" and "It looks like a tornado went through here"
I'm from Baptists, devoted and loving
I'm from Maryville, Tennessee
Fried chicken and mashed potatoes
From the brother who called himself "Coffee" and the aunt who travels the world
From shelves filled with scrapbooks, stuffed with old times and young faces, time to reminisce
I am from a country background, loud family members
And people I would never give away

Connor

I'm from front porches and lemonade

From sweet tea and guitars

I'm from the red brick farm house

Warm, friendly

It felt like home

I'm from lilac bushes and mountain laurel

Sweet smelling, pink blossoms

I'm from farming and hard work

From Paul and Mary and Tammy

I'm from football and Halloween

From promise and ingenuity

I'm from small, country churches with crosses

I'm from Tennessee

Sweet tea and chicken 'n dumplins

From the tenant farmers and the poor making their way

From one room concrete houses

I'm from farmers

I am from Tennessee

James

I'm from soccer balls

From Sony and Clorox

I'm from the house with the green roof and shutters and the light
brown siding

It felt warm and smooth

I'm from the green and pink and purple plants on the side of the
house

I'm from soccer traditions

From Amanda and Robert, Ronald and Kathleen

From the sport tendency and playing soccer

From "Don't talk to strangers" and "Look both ways before
crossing the road"

I'm from Christianity and Episcopalian

I'm from Knoxville, Tennessee

Fried chicken and turnip greens

From stories of hunting and fishing

I'm from soccer (that comes from my dad) and pictures that are
in my home

I'm from education and soccer

Haiku

James

Run as fast as possible!
Hurry up and run faster.
Don't ever slow down!

Run and kick the ball!
Kick the ball hard down the field.
Shoot and score a goal!

Salvador

I am from *Space Jam*

From Warner Brothers and Family Entertainment

I am from great white walls, big and strong

It felt safe and sturdy

I'm from football games every Saturday, and the enjoyment that
brings me

From Isabel and Sofia and Helena

I'm from amazing hamburgers and awesome steak

From "If at first you succeed, try not to look surprised" and "No
post on Sundays"

I'm from a Christian background, a believer in God

I'm from the United State of America and Spain

Tacos and burritos

I'm from the lottery winner who only won $100 and the son of a
billionaire

Memories stacked down the stairs and inside the garage

I am from Maryville, the vast town with bright lights

Eli

I am from Knoxville

From Nikki and Matt

I'm from the crazy and the silly

From "You were a boss" and "One day you will be a model"

I'm from Jesus and believe each man was born equal

I'm from ancestry of Scotland and England

From fish and deer meat

I'm from the time my great aunt and uncle met on their first
blind date

And the cabinets full of family photos from the great outdoors

I am from the place of the coolest

I am Eli

Allyson

I am from rowing oars

From plastic and rubber

I am from the old metal shed down by the water

Glistening, dusty, it looks like a bug graveyard

I am from the willow tree in the knee-high grass

Tall and looming over all who dare to wander too close

I am from family reunions and strong personalities

From Chris and Christine

I'm from the "Have one" or "Have none,"

From "Don't be stupid" and "Don't be afraid"

I'm from The Man who was hung on a cross

To save others from harm

I'm from Pennsylvania and Chris's branch

Corn and ice cream

From the ranch Bud built to have a home

The king of my father's wrestling team

Up in the attic stored safely away, to once again be remembered

I am from the strong-hearted and independent family, born and

grown in Iowa to expand across the world

Ramsey

I am from roots

From footballs and backyards

I am from the South, loving, and homegrown

It feels like your favorite pair of blue jeans

I am from mountain streams, clear and swift

From fireworks on the 4th of July and loving all

From Jill and Mike and Holly

I'm from the quick to make a joke and quick to help a friend

From Jesus loves me and Jesus loves the little children of the world

I'm from Fairview United Methodist Church and mission trips

I'm from "Murville," Tennessee and the Cherokee Nation

From Horn of Plenty and burgers off the grill

From the Sinks where Mom would jump off the rocks as a little girl

And the football game where Dad made his first touchdown catch

On the living room mantle are pictures

I am from Rocky Top, Tennessee

With great legends and inspiration just around the river bend

Kiersten

I'm from the mountains

From a barn and the country

I'm from the rolling hills of Tennessee

Green and large

Crisp air and cool breeze

I'm from dogwood trees and gardenia bushes, sweet and free

I'm from Christmas trees and cheery attitudes

From Karen and Chase and Kendra

I'm from athletic skills of my dad and the smart thinking of my

mom

I'm from "Quiet down" and "Work hard'

I'm from a Christian home, where church is every Sunday

I'm from Iowa

Corn and potatoes

From the ancestor that created hybrid corn

The hard working farmers harvesting crops

I'm from Maryville, Tennessee

I'm Kiersten

Krista

I am from an old film camera
From Kodak and Canon
I am from houses that stand firm of bricks
Strong, yet weak, it tasted of salt and vinegar
I am from dandelions, the weeds, beautiful, yet painful, I'm
happy to be
I remember as if they were my own
I'm from Friday night movies and the loud and argumentative
I'm from Pattersons turned Nolans and Scott and Karen
I'm from the loud and talkative, the ignorant and stubborn
From "Hit them with your best shot" and "Never say die"
I'm from confused, dazed, and the one who wonders why
I'm from the roots of America
Salads and takeout food
From stories of the lake and joyous Christmas gatherings
Down the hall, a little to the right, I'm from a place where
dreams do not thrive
But my own dreams and thoughts can't be held
A place where people can only dream to leave
And the great ones can follow their trains of thoughts
A place where color fades to tones of white and orange
A place where you are meant to leave to discover
And live for yourself

J.P.

I am from fishing rods

From Shakespeare and Shimano

I am from rocky foothills

Steep, red

It sounds alive

I am from great poplars and mighty oaks

Towering, ancient, strong

I'm from Sunday Dinners and forward-leaning walks

From Arnold Willie and Vivian Irene

I'm from "dust monkeys," loud laughers, and wood workers

From, "Spend less time talking, and more time doing" and

"Show some hustle!"

I'm from red, wooden pews and warm baptizing water

I'm from Maryville and France

Soup-beans and corn bread

From the long drive from Virginia to get married in Kentucky

The letters written to Fort Worth from Knoxville

The reels of memories in the upstairs bedroom

I am from the South

From Friday night football and Sunday morning church

Catherine

I am from clean sheets

From Mayfield and Lysol

I am from three stories of brick

Comfortable, familiar

It felt worn

I am from butterfly bushes and a dying oak, old and expansive

I'm from lighting candles and long feet

From Mark and Kelly and Nicholas

I'm from movement across states and alcoholism

From "Never complain" and "Always being thankful"

I'm from nondenominational Christianity, where we know that

Heaven exists

I'm from Knoxville and Ireland

Baked potatoes and American food

From the trip to Cabin 8, when we went tubing and my brother

flipped my grandfather

The affectionate heart of my grandmother

Memories on the mantle

I am from being alone and being happy about it

Amanda

I am from dishtowels and Ivory soap

I am from waves crashing onto the dock as the boats go by

Quiet, relaxing

It felt as if none of your worries would ever catch you

I am from pinecones and hydrangeas, sweet colorful clusters

I'm from bonfires and togetherness

From Cory and Daniel and Rocky

I'm from quiet storytelling and trips out to dinner

From "The Easter bunny coming" and Santa's big fat belly

I'm from church choir

Singing peacefully every Sunday

I am from Fayetteville, Georgia

Crab legs and shrimp

From hiking trips with my parents and almost getting eaten by a
bear

The multiple flips on the Jet Ski with my dad

Every picture hanging on the wall in the hall

I am from always being myself and telling the truth, no matter
how hard

Six Word Memoir

Matt

Measured by success, shaped by failures.

Ashlyn

I am from flower vases
From Polly Pockets and tea parties
I am from the giant oak tree with the tire swing dangling from its
limbs
Sturdy, massive
It felt like your worries were gone and flying was the only way
I am from zinnias and lightning bugs flashing all around
Going to church on Sunday and always being humble
From Mom and Dad, Gram and Gramps, Nana and Grandpa
I'm from potlucks and picnics
From "Yes ma'am" and "Yes sir" and "Never waste a dime"
I'm from Baptist churches and knowing Jesus as my Savior
I'm from the Great Smoky Mountains and the river behind the
mill
Grits and black coffee
From the food we are always cooking and the whole family
together on Thanksgiving

Haiku
Ashlyn

The water rushes

The current is very swift

It washes away

Memories will fade

And few will last forever

They will always count

Lauren

I am from bobby pins

From Crayola and Fisher-Price

I am from blades of grass beneath the Quince bushes

Coarse, stunted, they tasted like hay

I am from evergreens and Japanese maples in my grandmother's
yard

I'm from Sunday morning pancakes and thick eyeglasses

From Ernest and Charles and Diane

I'm from the procrastinators and over-achievers

From "See you in the morning light!" and "Sleep tight!"

I'm from Darwinism and Unitarian Universalist

I'm from Seattle and ancient Appalachia

Corn grits and kale

From the wedding ring my grandmother swallowed and the dorm
where my parents met

Above the cedar chest was a bookcase, its shelves held old photo
albums, a collage of lost faces

Speaking stories I'm too young to tell

I am from those fragments, snapshots of life before me, drops of
family history

Tyler

I am from Duct Tape

From Sharpie and Gerber

I am from the city of Rushford

Run down

It tasted like postage stamps

I am from the trees, the forest

Dark, green, fresh

I'm from procrastination

I am from birthdays and brown eyes

From Joan and Bryan and Peggy

Haiku

Tyler

Like a meadow we walk
With the flowers we stand and stare
Like the marshes we talk

The trees talk and wait
With the largest of all time
On the grassy plain

Jamie

I'm from computers that hum

From Hewlett-Packard and Adobe

I'm from white walls of comfort, caring, and gentle

It tastes like chocolate

I'm from tomato plants that grow and the sweet watermelons, green and striped

I'm from people who laugh

From Bonnie and David and John

I'm from habits, of chewing nails and being energetic

From "Look both ways before you cross the road" and "Always be nice to others"

I'm from church every Sunday and dressing lady-like

I'm from China, adopted

Beef dumplings and rice

From the time my grandfather broke his back and my grandfather who fought in a war

From a fireplace mantle packed with old pictures

I'm from white picket fences that sway in the breeze

Marie

I am from art
From Acrylic paint and cheap canvas
I am from the small brick house
From warm and cozy and quiet
I am from the willow tree
From the freshly cut green grass
From grass swaying in the breeze
I'm from the family that always blesses their food and takes care
of one another
From Meredith and Larry
From Matthew and Macie
I'm from the family that is loud and sometimes a bit obnoxious
From "Don't slouch. You'll ruin your back." and "Smile. It's
good for you."
I'm from going to church twice a year
From still worshipping The Lord every day
I'm from Signal Mountain, Chattanooga, Tennessee
From Germany and Sweden
From Swedish meatballs and homemade bread
From the annoying older brother that used to call me "Sissy"
From the granny that makes everything taste good
From the stack of old pictures on my dresser
I am from the loud, loving, warm, cozy, life

Brandon

I am from a big house in Northfield
I am from the big white house on the block with a pool, and a
big backyard
It looks like a big white marshmallow waterfall
I am from the flower
The flower of life, the red and white flower
I'm from the family gathering for Thanksgiving
And long hair
From games and food
From Bobby and Suzanne and Rusty
I'm from drinking Icees and eating
From "You will grow up to be something amazing" and "You
are perfect the way you are"
I'm from non-believers of religion and knowing that science can
explain everything
I'm from Blount Memorial Hospital
From a good family
I am from a gamer that loves his son

Zahraa

I am from Michael Jordan's shoe

From Nikes and Jordans

I am from a wood house

Warm and cozy

It tastes really sweet

I am from the rose that is pink

I am from a family that will always treat me as an expensive gift

A family that is nothing like the other families

From Shireen and Ahlam and Israa

I am from the sweet with kind hearts

A family that will never break apart

From a girl that looked nothing like the other girls and

Always stayed happy and cheerful

I am from the Muslims

Who really do respect women

I am from Iraq

Kebabs and Falafels

From the way my little sister dances

And the way my older sister dreams of success

I am a person who will never give up

No matter how hard life gets

A Letter to Myself

Zahraa

Dear Me,

      Here I am sitting in a lovely room next to the lovely Noah. The friends I have right now I would never want to replace ever in my life. It is so amazing that I have them in my life. I also have the most amazing family in the world they treat me in the best way. I am always fighting with my older sister, Shireen, well we are not really fighting we are bickering it's like arguing but cuter. My younger sister, Israa, is the cutest thing is the world, it is so sad watching her grow up, I want her to stay 1 forever and never get older. Maybe in the future the will create a magical water that will make you stay at a certain age forever Bottom of line is that I may be living the best time of my life right now, but maybe I will have a better life in the future, but the life I have right now is amazing, yes it could be hard sometimes, but that's what life is, facing the challenges.

Kevin

I am from a bar of soap
From Dove and Axe
I am from the bathtub full of water, blue and refreshing
It looked like a witch's boiling cauldron
And tasted like hot dry bread
I am from the dove shaped flower
The flower smells just how I smell
I'm from the celebration of Christmas and Greek Khakis
From Julie and Kevin and Toby
I'm from the forgetful family and generations of Kevins
From a factory that makes chemicals
From religions that are more creative than the one I am in now
I'm from North Dakota: September 22, 1999
From Taco Bell and Domino's
From the person that died before Christmas
From pictures on the fridge
20% Greek from the Khakis
From beliefs, Christian based

Poem to my Future self in Haiku form

Kevin

The past is too easy

The present will get more advanced

The future is only technology

Maggie

I am from bicycles

From Toys-R-Us and tap shoes

I am from the concrete driveway in front of the house

Hot, gray

It always had chalk on it

I am from the sand on the beach

The cool glistening water from the ocean

I am from the Playbills and Metro cards

From Heidi and Jon

I am from the loudmouths and the outspoken ones

From "Clean your room" and "We're moving again"

I am from the Kingdom Hall and all the Bible books

I'm from Hawaii and New Jersey

Tacos and guacamole

From the bus that my dad rode every morning to go into the city
and work, where he would pass all the skyscrapers and pizza
restaurants

I'm from the winter mornings where the four-foot-deep white
snow would wake me

Six Word Motto

Andrew

Snowboarding is a way of life.

Alex

I am from the microwave

From Samsung and Pepsi

I am from the white house with three stories

Tall, it looked different

I am from the Venus Fly Trap, sharp and dangerous

I'm from the Christmas Eve dinners, brown hair and blue eyes

From Steve and Rebecca and Judy

I'm from watching Tennessee football and going to the beach

From "Go Vols!" and "Stay in school"

I'm from a representation of Christianity

Jesus Christ died on the cross

I'm from Maryville, Tennessee

Cheeseburgers and hot dogs

From the Grandmother who won tickets twice

The grandfather who owns Misty Meadow driving range

From pictures on the tops of the shelves in the kitchen

I am from a die-hard Vol fan who loves music and Maryville

Six Word Mottos

Alex

When nothing goes right, go left.

I would rather be home sleeping.

Life can get rough, just persevere.

Something we all go through, school.

You can always overcome the odds.

When in doubt, listen to music.

Katy

I am from water, from flippers and chlorine

I am from the grass struggling to grow

Dark green and fresh, it felt like a soft bed

I am from the sky

The clouds whose dark gray wisps tell a story of a great battle

I am from fudge at Christmas and stubborn smarts

From Markay and Joyce and Jackson

I am from good grades and August fasts

From, "Make your bed!" and, "Clean your room!"

I am from God's perfect creation

A sacrifice that gives me hope

I'm from Europe, Asia, and North Carolina

Aunt Sally's lumpia and morning tea

From the pinkie that was chopped off my dad's hand in the

slammed door and the first broken bone in my sister's arm

I am from photos in the closet, packed for moving

Memories that had been forgotten

I am from wishing to do everything, wanting more time

And hoping for things to be right

Zach

I am from music and math

I am from Old Spice and the Valley of the Shadow of Death

I am from the scenery of the creek

I am the good, the bad, and the pretty

I am from the "Pretty Patties"

The pretty plants

I am from the pretty plastic llama in my yard

I am from Kool-Aid stands and the eating of food

I'm from Mommy and Daddy

I'm from the eating of food with my family

Sleeping in a bed

I'm from the "Don't have Sex" speech

I'm from Jesus

I'm from England

From poking of my grandfather's eye

From the Coca-Cola secrets

I AM FROM SPARTAAAAAAAAAAAAA!!!!!!

Haiku

Zach

The pretty llama

Likes pretty butterflies and

Pretty patties swag

The ROM has Rosen

I worship the ROM daily

THE ROM HAS ROOOSEEEEENNNNNNNN

Toly

I am from stoves and ovens

From Greek Gods and Kolios

I am from the Green paint and gardens

Soft, lush

They tasted juicy, sweet, and spicy

I am from the sunflowers, the sunflower so yellow and tall,

following the sun all day

I'm from the cooks and loudmouths

From George and Maria and Apostolos

I'm from the over-exaggerators and caretakers

From "Try your best!" and "Stop touching him!"

I'm from Orthodox worship

And lamb on Easter

I'm from Knoxville, Tennessee and Greece

From baklava and moussaka

From the family my grandmother lost to the Nazis

From the journey my great-grandfather made to America

I'm from the picture books on the shelves under the stairs

I am from home cooking

I am from Greece

Six Word Memoir

Toly

Get up, school, homework, bed, repeat.

Haiku

Joshua

The wind moves slowly

The grass dances in the wind

The breeze is life

It can bend the land

It can change history

Water is power

Jacob

I am from communication

From cell phones and touch screens

I am from the two story house, advanced and modern

It feels like the circuit boards and sounds like audio

I am from silicon, the ore of the future

I'm from the big Friday night games and bravery

From Jon and Donna and the one and only Creator

I'm from the church goers and sit down dinner attendees

From "No don't touch that" and "Do as I say not as I do"

I'm from Sunday mornings and Wednesday night youth group

I'm from Ireland, potatoes and corn

From the journey Great-granddad Wall endured

to arrive at the melting pot

From the farming and hardship set forth by the land

From the fire safe full of family members from the past

I am from the time of future endeavors where everything is

automatic

Drew

I am from soccer,

From Nike and Oakley

I am from the medium sized house with a red truck

It smells like Doritos, and sounds like music

I am from the Smoky Mountains and its trees

White in the winter, green in the summer

Multi-colored in the fall

I am from the Zacharias family and brilliant minds

From John and Gus and Monica

I am from travels to Colorado, California, D.C., Florida, Georgia

And back to Tennessee

From a land of greatness

I am from the almighty God

From great faith

I am from Maryville, Tennessee

Six Word Motto

Andrew

Improvising, working hard, leads to success.

Logan

I am from the piano
From Yamaha and Steinway and Sons
I am from the brick on the house
Rough, dark red
It feels like sandpaper
I am from the Sage Brush, the Calochortus nuttallii
White and pink petals
I am from cutting down Christmas trees
And arthritis
From John and Peterson and Kim
I'm from the smart alecks and the debaters
From "What you talkin' bout Willis?" and "Stop doing that!"
I'm from the Latter-Day Saints
The Restored Church on the Earth
I'm from California and Cherokee
Squash and fish
From the guy who walked on moving trains and planes
And the person who gave my family the Bollwinkel name
I am from Disneyland, my second home
The place where I know people

Angelina

I am from pointe shoes
From Grishko and Freed
I am from the spiders crawling under the door
Black, dreary; they looked humane
I am from the daisies, from the swaying trees, whose leaves
stretch like a ballerina's frail arms on stage
I am from merging cultures and big, green eyes
From Ivan and Maxim and Maria
I am from the taut conversations and from painstakingly loud
nights
From making good grades and from keeping fake friends
I am from big, elaborate churches
From Russian Orthodox in Ust-Labinsk
From always being watched
I am from a small town, but I am from big people
From borscht and fresh bread
From the engagement party for Ivan
From new Aunt Inna
From the deep brown hair and the kind smile
I am from the Black Sea
From the cold, clean water
I am from the stage
From always dancing, dancing, dancing

From almost (but not quite) flying away

Chad

I am from Fishing

From hunting and trucks

I am from the woods

From the smell of dust

I'm from the sound of the clock

It felt like a home

I am from an apple

The sunflower, yellow

I'm from hunting and fishing

From Grandpa

I'm from Godliness, good grades, and family

From Thomas the Tank Engine and

Bob the Builder

I'm from God and Christianity

I'm from my grandfather's Indian tribe

Pinto beans and cornbread

From my Great-Grandfather's WWII experience

From meat eaters at the grill

I am from a mountain that has not been conquered yet

Six Word Motto

Chad

You catch some and you lose some.

Brianna

I am from the radio that blasts music 24/7
From a Crayola Crayon box
I am from the brown house with the squeaky doors
I am from the beautiful and bright Hibiscus
The brightness of the sun
I am from every birthday spent at Grandma's house
From brown eyes
From Amanda and a father I missed
And a family with different last names
I am from the family that talks much and speaks its mind
From "Respect is earned not given" and "If you don't have
anything nice to say, don't say anything at all"
I am from a family of Christians and the Bible knows best
I'm from Chicago, Illinois and Maryville, Tennessee
From rice and beans
From the trips to Mexico, the almost getting lost, and the
Pittsburg visits
I am from a box in the basement with all our memories and
achievements

Nicholas

I am from pizza
From Papa Johns and Pizza Hut
I am from a warm and elegant mansion, formed into a mere two
stories
Massive, yet small house feeling,
Loving and showing of interests displayed in every room
It sounds quiet and feels comfy
I am from sunflowers and snap dragons
Bright, yellow, tall, and beautiful
Full of life, seeing what eyes can't and feeling what fingers and
toes cannot begin to understand
I'm from church and ears that turn red for no reason
I'm from Patrick, Kristy, and Ginger
From intelligent, respectful, and religious
From "If you eat the seeds, a watermelon will grow in your
stomach" and "Black cats are bad luck" and "Treat your
neighbor like yourself"
I'm from Sunday school with coloring books, graham crackers,
and apple juice
I believe in the one true King, Father, Son and Holy Spirit
I'm from the "dawg" house where football is key
The land of *Braveheart* a lineage of Wallaces
Seafood, caught fresh from the sea

Loaves of bread, fresh from the oven

Eaten when times were good

From a poor family with five sons, two of whom died in a fire

And heartbreaks of another saddened age, located in dusty scrapbooks and abandoned spaces

I am from places in which many have stood with honor

From respecting all people

From the privilege of being an Army brat

From meeting people that have been through hell and back and lived to tell the tale

I'm from feeling honored to be free in the great country for which my ancestors fought

Limericks

Nicholas

I once ate a ginormous apple pie
So big it touched the sky
I am not feeling so well, I must rebuke
I think I might puke, so goodbye!

My ears are so great
They don't really work, but wait
At least I have my chocolate cake
For goodness sake
Why am I eating this so late?

Rebekah

I am from Chacos

From Vera Bradley and Nike

I'm from a small brick home, light brown, welcoming, it sounds
like the wind

I am from flowers and green trees

From family Thanksgiving dinner and blue eyes

From Deborah and Eric and Mary

I'm from foreigners and followers

From "Be happy!" and "Follow your dreams!"

I'm from the Bible, the Ten Commandments

I'm from Youngstown, Ohio, and Croatia

Walnut rolls and stuffed cabbage

From the great-grandmother who sailed from the Ukraine to
New York when she was thirteen

And the great-grandmother born in Croatia

On my bookshelf in a photo album where many wonderful
memories are held

I am from wonderful moments of memories, a leaf from my
family tree

Haiku

Rebekah

"Leaves"

Falling and turning

Colors orange and yellow

Bring beauty to the fall

"Flower"

Growing and blooming

Soaking up all the sunshine

Beauty to the spring

Leah

I am from dog leashes

From Chacos and Mary Kay

I am from the gray house with a pool

Glimmering, cozy, it smelled like watermelon lemonade

I am from hibiscus and the poplar tree whose limbs are strong
and sturdy

I am from evening swims and comforting smiles

From Rick and Christine

I'm from cooks and hard workers

From "Leave that alone!" and "Don't touch that."

I'm from "He leads me beside still waters" and the Ten
Commandments

I'm from China

Coffee and raspberries

From Myrtle Beach trips, riding in a golf cart

The sweetness and warmth

In the storage box in the corner of my parents' bedroom lies old
memorable pictures

I am from Maryville, Tennessee

Winning football, tall trees, and gorgeous mountains

Dana

I am from hairbrushes

From Conair and Goody

I am from a house, comfy and brown, it feels like home to me

I am from flowers and trees that bloom in my backyard

I am from family dinners and birthday parties

From Mom and Dad

I am from shopping at the grocery store and going on vacation

From "Do good" and "Follow the rules"

I am from Florida

Chicken and pasta

I am from fingers my dad lost to a saw

And meals we all have together

A drawer in my room holds all the pictures of my family and me

I am from experiences of what has happened

And dreams of what is to come

"School: Fall and Summer"

Dana

Whenever fall comes

Students start to gather near

Filling halls with cheer

Summer is coming

The halls will soon be empty

Hear the students cheer

Nicole

I am from peaches

From Coca-Cola and Chick-fil-a

I am from the sunny brick house

It felt warm

I am from Quercus Virginiana, the Cherokee rose

Derived from the Cherokee Indians who distributed the plant

I'm from baklava every Christmas and tiny hands

From Cheryl and David and Cara

I'm from talkative and humorous

From "Most of your heat leaves through your head" and

"Brussels sprouts are good"

I'm from Christianity and Germany

Bratwurst and sauerkraut

From alien autopsy t-shirts, the chromed locker in an album

I am from the computer

Haiku

Nichole

Autumn pumpkin spice
Halloween is on its way
Only one more month

The screen's bright white glare
In the darkness of midnight
The gamer plays on

Ashton

I am from baseball

From Purina puppy food and Domino's pizza

I am from mountainous Smokies

From the rushing water of the Tennessee River

I am from dogwoods, and vibrant, purple irises

I'm from the Iron Bowl on the third Saturday in October

From Neal and Sandy and Grandma Wallace

I'm from the world where all animals are pets and screaming for
no reason

From movies all night long and playing all day long

From a world where "Nothing is perfect" and "Mom is always
right"

I am from church every Sunday morning

And again every Sunday night

I am from Maryville and Scotland

From War Eagle and "Go Vols", From AU and UT

I'm from camping

Chicken nuggets and pizza

From the "smart" mastering student, the lifesaving parent, and
the pet-loving mom

I am from trips Disney and sandy beaches, and familiar bike
rides among wildlife

I'm a boy who can hardly ask to be from more

Haiku

Ashton

I like to play games
I like to eat pizza and cake
I like to go fishing

I like to eat food
I like to go to Football games
I like to go golfing

Emma

I am from violins

From rosin and Baroque

I'm from the concealed house, medium, hidden, scented with
Snuggle

I am from rose bushes, bright with red roses

From yearly get-togethers and tempers

From Caroline and Vicki

I'm from know it all's and musicians

From "Be yourself" and "Act like an adult"

I'm Catholic, church class every Wednesday

From Maryville, Tennessee

Pizza and cookies

From summer beach trips with fun, arguments, late night girl
talks with cousins, and weekly visits to my grandparent's house

I am from scrapbooks full of pictures, letters written to my
grandfather

And memories that will never go away

Most Memorable Moment

Emma

My most memorable moment was when I made Jr. Clinic in orchestra. I've been playing the violin since fifth grade and in seventh grade, orchestra students had the opportunity to audition for Jr. Clinic which is only available for seventh, eighth, and ninth graders. If you make it in, you go to a selected school on Friday and Saturday and practice all day. Saturday you have a concert in the afternoon. It was my first year auditioning and I was really nervous. I didn't think I would get in even though I constantly practiced until my fingers hurt. We had to play a prepared piece and two scales for the judges. It was a blind audition, so the judges couldn't actually see you which made it a little better. I knew our teacher had prepared us, but I was still nervous. I remember I was shaking when I went in to audition and my heart was beating so fast. I was nervous when I was playing the scales which came first, but after I got the feel of what it was like, I realized it wasn't that bad. After I finished, I actually felt confident. Then came the sight reading. If I struggle with one thing in orchestra, it's sight reading. Sight reading is when you get a piece of music, usually not more than half a page long, and you have one minute to look at it until you have to play it for the judges. What makes it hard is that you have never seen the piece and you can't make any sound or you will be deducted points. After the minute is up, you have to play it for the judges. I remember the piece we had to sight read was really hard with confusing rhythms and high notes. Any confidence I had completely vanished after that. When I left, I was relieved that it was over, but I was really anxious to get the results. Our teacher said that he would email us the results once he got them. I was literally checking my email every five minutes that day. Finally, after what seemed like forever, I found out that I had gotten in! I was so excited, proud, relieved, and glad that I had the courage to even try out. I am usually quiet and shy, but I feel like when I play the violin I can challenge myself to be louder and braver. Making Jr. Clinic boosted my self-confidence so much and I continue to try out two years later. In eighth grade I tried out and made it, and I am actually about to try out again in ninth. Playing an instrument has taught me many things, but the most I have learned is having courage and more confidence.

Will

I am from huge yards
From burgers and fries
I am from the white house in the middle of nowhere that's beside
a barn
It smells like a farm
I am from a big oak tree in front of my yard
From traditions like opening one present on Christmas Eve
I'm from athletic brothers
From Luke and Seth and Alesia
A hardworking and loyal family, from being a rock and an
athlete
I'm from Christians who attend services as much as possible
I'm from Maryville
Carrot cake and banana puddin'
From little brother Seth, who gained the nickname "the buckling
king" because, if one of the people in my family wasn't buckled
in his seatbelt, he'd cry, "Buckle huckle!"
I'm from an older brother who became the kicker for the high
school football team and earned the nickname "Kicker"
I'm from pictures and memories at the beach
I am from a white house, two brothers, and an amazing mom

Gabriella

I am from the cherry blossom tree with flowers drifting down
From Miracle Grow and Peters' soil
I am from the big house with fences for protection
It sounded creaky and looked big
I am from a black rose and sunflowers without any seeds
Small, shy, yet beautiful
I'm from Mexicans, Americans, and brown eyes
From Maria and Javier
From quiet and outgoing
I am from non-church going Christians
From Mexico and America
Tamales and hamburgers
From the death of an overdose while lying in bed, the broken and
the dead
Ugly places you'd never expect to be so beautiful
I am from depression and happiness
From liars and truth tellers

Christian

I am from soft drinks

From Coca-Cola and Dr. Pepper

I am from a perfect place

The backyard, all night parties

It looks, sounds, and feels like perfection

I am from trees, leaves, sticks and stems

I'm from the Volunteers and huge ears

From Bud and Tracy and Mimama

I'm from never sleeping and always arguing

From perseverance and effort

I'm from Sunday School, early morning, long-lasting Sunday
school

I'm from Chattanooga

French fries and Italian pies

From airplane fliers like Weldon and marching band majors like
John

From the beach

I am from Heaven

Morgan

I am from sweet tea

From Minute Maid and Mayfield

I am from the two story neighborhood hub

Beautiful, big

It felt like a spring day

I am from tulips and oak trees, hose shade stretches across the
front yard

I'm from fudge at Christmas time and eyeglasses

From Melba and Don and Billy

I'm from outgoing and Christ loving

From "Always work hard" and "Always eat fruits and
vegetables"

I'm from Jesus is my Savior, and memorizing 20 Bible verses
for a prize

I'm from Maryville and Paducah

Barbeque and black coffee

From the arm my great-grandfather lost and the prosthetic knees
that allowed my grandfather to walk

From my grandmothers antique cabinet with too many photo
albums and boxes

Overflowing with memories

I'm from the God-loving family nestled in a small town under the Great Smoky Mountains

Limericks
Morgan

There once was a girl with sweet tea.

She said, "This is perfect for me!"

Two glasses later,

She asked the nice waiter,

"Could you give me another one, please?"

It is now the season of fall.

Are you ready for some football?

It comes Friday night,

To students' delight,

There is excitement and fun for all.

Garrett

I am from football
From MoonPies and *The Body Farm*
I'm from red bricks and white siding, comfort and joy, it feels
warm
I am from iris, the Liriodendron tulipifera, green, brown, and
carbon dioxide absorbing
Thanksgiving with the entire family and tall stature
From Dalton and Logan and Lori
I'm from the tall and athletic
From Santa is real and so is the Easter Bunny
I'm from the stereotypical Baptist, "… and if you don't do this
then, that's a sin and that is wrong and blah, blah, blah…"
I'm from Germany
Sauerkraut and Schnitzel
From the kid who almost lost his finger when he was chasing a
groundhog and the girl that was so excited for Thanksgiving
dinner that she almost cut off her finger with the turkey knife
I am from Tennessee
I'm 15, a swimmer, and most importantly, I am me

Skyler

I am from books

From Marvel and Nesquick

I am from a hammock on the back porch

Comfortable, peaceful, it felt magical

I am from irises and weeping willows whose long mosses

comfort my soul

I'm from Litchfield visits and blue eyes

From Sarah and Matt and Lynn

I'm from a running and traveling family

From "You can do anything you put your mind to" and "Always

do your best and you will succeed"

I'm from Catholicism

The Father, The Son, and The Holy Ghost

I'm from Knoxville and Ireland, Germany and Scotland

Sauerkraut and mash

From the airplane my great-grandfather built and flew by hand

From the cancer that did not take my grandmother

On top of the bookshelves are many framed memories of my

whole family

I am from persistence and perseverance of all things that I face

Madison

I am from cute clothes

From tank tops and t-shirts

I am from laundry

It smelled clean

It felt soft

I am from wild morning glories and tulips, red and pretty

I'm from wrestling

From people who are crazy, tall, and smart

Michelle and Drew and Linda

I'm from "Always focus on your work" and "Always work hard"

I'm from Christians, from Baptists

From Knoxville, Tennessee

Spaghetti and pizza

From shopping trips with Mom and getting slushies with

Grandmother

I'm from pictures taken at my grandparents' house

I am a sweet, sensitive, and shy girl

Olivia

I am from Microsoft Windows
From Nutella and iPod
I am from rocking chairs on the front porch, it felt light and airy
It smelled of freshly cut grass
I am from honeysuckle vines
And the cherry blossom tree whose twisting trunks I learned by
heart
I'm from M-shaped mouths and long legs
From Malerie and Hannah and Beth
I'm from stubborn and hard headed
From "Stay still!" and "Be quiet!"
I'm from songs of The Lord Almighty
And the Savior who saved us all
I'm from Rocky Top in Volunteer Nation
Fried chicken and potato salad
From the foot my mother broke walking down bleachers
The Guatemalan coffee my sister gave to my father from a
mission trip
From pictures scattered around the house, in every little nook
and niche
The best and worst of us

I am from sleepless nights, jumping hay bales, and baking rough skin in humid summers

Six Word Memoir
Olivia

Life was one big panic attack.

Jake

I am from Maryville, Tennessee
Baseball gloves and basketballs
I am from the old brick house
Two floors with four bedrooms
It felt natural, of baked clay, a material once found in the ground
I'm from Thanksgiving dinners
From athletic family members
From Michael and Andrew and Rosanna
I'm from happiness and friendliness
From "I hope you get caught if you do something bad" and
"Always do your best"
I'm from Christianity
Jesus saves all
I'm from Knoxville, Tennessee
And Portugal, Brazil, and England
Crepes and English tea
From Dad working all summer to earn enough money to buy a
TV to watch Tennessee football games
The same Dad who now takes me to UT home games
From the storage building where the family pictures are
I am from the small town, Maryville, Tennessee

Meredith

I am from a frayed December Southern Living magazine
From mediocre homemade holiday wreaths and classic recipes
I am from pressed Sunday dresses and patent leather shoes
From creamy lace trimmed socks and golden hair tied up in
ribbons
I am from two bedroom Victorian homes, delicate and pristine
From the antique claw foot bathtub and the yellowing curtains in
the parlor
I am from a chilling cello suite in G, from heavy viscosity,
gliding off the strings
I am from the live oak in the back yard
From age old branches reaching up, up, up until they scrape the
soft September sky
I am from lazy ten o'clock Saturday breakfasts
From the sun filtered in through the curtains on the big picture
window
I am from the aroma of brewing coffee
I am from busy Monday mornings, fumbling to get ready
I am from Christmas Eve mass at the Episcopal Church
From the eleven o'clock black-as-spilled-ink sky
I am from the Holy Eucharist, from "Go in peace to love and
serve the Lord"

I am from the serenity that follows the service

From the blanket of snow that envelops the word in a frosty calm

I am from Libby's house on Second Street, beloved palmetto trees lining the yard

I am from the Gulf Coast, salt in the air and clammy sunshine on my face

I am from brunch at a Sardis Huddle House with Granddaddy

From golden brown waffles smothered in strawberries and whipped cream

I am from thick, curly hair and Mama's Coca-Cola cake

From stubborn mothers and calm fathers

I am from black picture frames on buttery yellow walls

From bittersweet memories like the first bite of a cool key lime pie

I am from, most of all, a love that goes back generations

From this love, I find home

To the Little Girl Waiting by the Window
Meredith

Dear little girl, waiting by the window. Elbows resting on the sill, sleepy smile on your face. Rise with the sun on every Tuesday morning, wave to the neighbors and the drowsy garbage men. They see you shining bright like the orange sunrise. Keep love in your heart.

Dear little girl in the floppy straw hat, green pajamas on and your tiny feet are bare. Dance across the porch until your corkscrew hair runs wild. Mama's on her toes and Daddy's out of breath. Keep love in your heart.

Dear little girl in the pink leotard, crooked tutu on your hips, sly smile on your lips. Your balance may be off, but what is there to fix? Don't stop twirling, and giggling, and giving hugs around the neck. Keep love in your heart.

Dear little girl in the itchy blue sweater, hold your sister in your arms, touch her soft rosy cheeks. Brown eyes are screwed shut as she grabs your little finger. She's glowing and she's warm, and she's yours to protect. Keep love in your heart.

Dear little girl in the red velvet dress, golden curls, hazel eyes, with rosy cheeks to match. Your grin stretches wide, throw your head back with a laugh. Spin in your dress, laugh when you trip. Keep love in your heart.

Dear sleepy girl in the room with yellow walls. Fall asleep to passing cars and a classical cassette. Close your eyes, rest your head, and curl up in your bed. Love is in your heart.

Sleep now, and wake up to wait by the window again.

Brennan

I am from Mason jars
From Old Spice and Crest
I am from the dirt on the floor from the dogs, brown, moist, it
felt dirty
I am from oak trees, creeks in the mountains, cold as ice
From Christmas Eve gatherings and chaotic cousins
From Stacy and Matt and Connor
I'm from the soccer family and beach trips
From ABCs and 123s
I'm from Christian faith and praying before dinner
From St. Mary's Hospital and Knoxville
Pecan pie and figs
From the corny jokes my grandfather tells, the story of my father
and the jar of moonshine
I'm from the shelf of scrapbooks my grandmother made
Bundled memories for me to keep
I am from "Murvul," Tennessee
Barbecues and football games

Six Word Memoirs

Brennan

I have time to fix this.

I'd rather be playing my cello.

The least important word is I.

Tick. Tock. Tick. Time is wasting.

No, I'm not in the band.

Carmen

I am from books

From Barnes & Noble and Amazon

I am from the humble abode

Comfortable, true, and familiar

I am from the willow tree

Quiet and proud

I'm from Frisbee games and brown eyes

From Marva and Eric and Reed

I am from pretty cool and funny

From quiet Christianity and dinner prayer

I'm from Knoxville

From Germans and native Alabamians

Corned beef and blueberry pie

From the insane horse girls and cat attacks

Memories stored in the huge box in the closet

I am from the hippie city and suburban town

A screened in porch and a window seat

Lexi

I am from tall vases

From Crayola crayons and Barbie dolls

I am from the big living room

Crazy colors that glistened when the sun hit them

They made me feel like I was a bird in a rose garden

I am from violets and tall trees whose leaves and long branches
reminded me of a human swaying in the wind

I'm from Christmas movies and funny jokes

From Frances and David

I'm from loud mouths and know-it-alls

From "No running in the house!" and "You could argue with a
wall!"

I'm from "Jesus loves you", and the memory verses I never seem
to forget

I'm from Maryville and Scotland,

Corn on the cob and pinto beans

From the tattoos my siblings got secretly and the concussions my
brother had every other week

The family photos stored away in photo albums, with the happy
faces smiling through family adventures

I am from a family full of love and support

And a community of people who will always have my back

Memorable Moment

Lexi

There is only one memory I have that I would count as my most memorable moment. That is the moment I found out I was going to have a niece. I was eleven years old and had just gone to a school dance when my parents told me. I got in the car and my mom said "So, your sister is pregnant." I just sat there for a second and then I was finally like wait I am going to have a niece or nephew! I was so excited. My sister took my mom and me with her to find out what the baby was, and when we found out it was a girl, I was so excited! My niece is going to turn three in November, and she is one of my favorite people ever. A few weeks ago, my sister told us that she is pregnant with her second child. I cannot wait until that little angel comes into the world, and I know I will love him or her very much.

Logan

I'm from books

From Disney movies and Star Wars toys

I'm from the playroom in my basement

Wood panels and brown carpet

From the huge pine tree in my backyard and helicopters falling

off my grandma's tree

I'm from holiday meals and curly hair

From Savannah, Cheyenne, and Caleb

I'm from lively storytellers and intelligent introverts

From "Don't spin around in circles" and "Try new things"

I'm from Pecks Memorial, Fairview United Methodist, and

Carpenters, choir and Bible school

From Ireland and Maryville

Cornbread and mac 'n cheese

From the time Cheyenne ate blue play dough and Nana dressed

like a ghost

From pictures on top of the TV, reminding me of the past

I'm from my house on Ray and my grandparents' houses

Where I became who I am today

Jordan

I am from cold soda
From Papa Murphy's and Little Caesar's
I am from temperatures of 108 degrees
Fire and humidity, it felt damp all the time
I am from magnolia blooms and pinecones
On the ground during fall
I'm from Christmas Eve services and freckled, brown-eyed girls
From Angela and Robert and Hailey
I'm from noisy and boldly spoken opinions
From "Do as I say, not as I do" and "Because I said so"
I'm from church on Sunday and volunteer until you run out of
things to do
I'm from the Bible belt
French fries and catfish
From the family with a twin known as the "invisible child"
The sister of a know it all
I am from the family who loves you too
Much for your own good
And a little girl who never could keep her mouth shut

Six Word Memoirs

Jordan

I've changed so much since then.

FC is love, FC is life.

Leann

I am from sports

From World Cups and exercising

I am from the boonies

Quiet

I am from the sunflower

Yellow and happy

I'm from staying up on Christmas Eve

From brown eyes and black hair

From Haldo and Silvia and Jenny

I'm from being short in stature and joking

From "Santa Claus is real" and "There are no monsters under your bed"

I'm from God and His Son

I'm from Atlanta

Rice and avocado

From the story of how my parents met and the memories of my uncles and dad

Family pictures above the fire place

I am from joking around, working out, and chilling out

Gavin

I am from consoles

From Xbox One and PlayStation Four

I am from cozy, warm and toasty

I am from the flower, colorful

I'm from cooking out

And brown hair

From Kelly and Allen and Abram

I am from Christmas and Thanksgiving

From being all being together

From "Sit down and be quiet"

I'm from Christianity

Praying

Pizza and home cooked meals

I'm from going to the beach with my grandparents and going to

Dollywood with my parents

I am from Maryville, Tennessee

Jakob

I am from dirt

From Nike and Under Armour

I am from the trailer, white, small

It looked like a regular trailer

I am from the woods, the grass, green

I'm from Christmas and funniness

From Trey and Charlene and Charles

I'm from funny and tough

From "You can be anything" and "I believe in you"

I'm from Christian

From Houston, Missouri

Pizza and chicken

From Trey, my favorite uncle, who is only five years older than I

am

And his wife

They go on every trip with us

I am from Missouri

I am whoever I want to be

Lexie

I am from the Mockingbird State
From Micky D's Sweet Tea and a southern violin
I am from the blue grass of my clean and cozy home
It sounds like loud barking dogs and smells delicious
I am from irises, daisies, and oak trees
From hanging out with family on holidays and going to my
uncle's house on Thanksgiving
From Cindy and Chris and Marie
I'm from huge appetites and Friday night football
From "Stay away from strangers" and "Stay away from boys"
I'm from Christianity, church on Sundays
I'm from Maryville, Tennessee
Pumpkin pie and hash brown casserole
From the time my aunt and uncle thought that "dash of pepper"
was "dash pepper"
From my Mamaw Marie eating a slice of pumpkin pie on the
way to my uncle's house
I'm from pictures on the table, over the fireplace, and on the
walls
I am from not enduring tornadoes
I am from the country

Haiku of Fall

Lexie

Wind was getting cold
Then I knew fall was just ahead
Leaves turning colors

As I walk leaves crunch
Wearing furry grey ugg boots
Warm coffee at home

Ali

I am from food

From TYR and Ariat

I am from crazy and funny

Sounds really weird

I am from the rose that comes from the soil and smells so good

I'm from wild and crazy

From Cassidy and Hanna and Jim

I'm from loud but sincere

From Santa Claus and the Tooth Fairy

I'm from Jesus, who made me who I am today

I'm from Maryville

Burritos and rice

From the Indians who roamed the land

And Marcie

Our history hangs in the long hallway

Past to the present

I am from bravery, love, and trust in all ways

Haley

I am from iPods

From Nintendo and GameCube

I am from the brick house at the end of the street

The house on the hill

With the blue spruce

I am from the Indian tree

The timeworn tree that holds my swing

Ancient and old

I'm from the massive feasts

From Rick and Paula

And Courtney

From the belief in Heaven

And God

I'm from intense Catholicism

Church every Sunday

I'm from Maryville

Steak and hamburgers

I'm from all my dad's stories of when he was young

From his love for hiking and the Smokies

I, too, am from the Smoky Mountains

I am from an intense love for fiction

Scotty

I am from the apple tree
A tree with apples stemming off
I am from the apple seeds
And leaves
They taste like citrus
I'm from Knoxville
Southern growing
I'm from sledding and tanned skin
From Nikki and Dad
And Randy
I'm from the South and southern accents
From "Be a leader" and "Do what you're told"
I'm from vacation Bible school
Christianity
I'm from America
Apple pie and deep fried food
From the Indian native and Indian hunters
The Randy with dark skin
I am from Baptist Hospital
I'm from Knoxville, Tennessee

Indianna

I'm from where my soul sprouted

Rickety front porch rocking chairs

Honda motorcycles and Belk church dresses

I am from the rumbling of the motorcycle engine and warm hugs
waiting at the door

A classic household filled with laughter and love

As my laughter echoed down the hall it sounded like pure joy

I am from the seed of God's hand

And the first delicate flower of spring, blooming and brilliant

I'm from the hard headed and hard working

From Janet, LeAnn and Curtis Lee

From kind-hearted grandparents

I'm from the tempered and tender

From old wise tales and elderly childhood stories

I'm from a Heavenly Father looking down upon us with gracious
love and mercy

I'm from southern heat

Greasy baked beans and creamy mashed potatoes

From the 80's rock and roll my dad grew up and lived on

And my mother's primed, volumized hair

I'm from leaves falling all around and the smell of the crisp,
clean air

The collision of two different ways that merged together to form the customs of family

Rebecca

I am from Chacos
From Tre'semme shampoo and Bath and Body Works soaps
I am from flowers in the garden, colorful, fragrant
They felt soft under my feet
I am from rose bushes and Japanese cherry blossoms
Satisfying fragrances
I'm from sausage balls on Christmas morning
And freckles
From Jerry and Dana and Thomas and Jacob
I'm from athletics and laughter
From "Pride comes before a fall" and
"If you spend money, you don't save money"
I'm from Vacation Bible School and mission trips
From Mississippi and Birdwell's Branch
Corn and coffee
From the "jacked up" toenail my intelligent Granddaddy got
from the lawnmower
And my Papaw's shaking his head because of lightning
On the wall pictures hang, embedded with memories
I am from perseverance and always trying to do my best

Haiku

Rebecca

This is who I am
From my youth to teenage years
Older years to come

Mississippi State
Bulldogs to Tennessee Vols
This is where I'm from

Evan

I am from Maryville and Knoxville

I am from the South

Awesome, and fun

I'm from mountains; they are grand

From football on Saturdays and church on Sundays

From Kathryn and Doug and Ryan

I am from the humorous

I'm from people who want to win

From "Do good" and "Be respectful"

I'm from waking up early on Sundays and going to church

I'm from Knoxville and Bob

Corn and peas

From smashing fingers in car doors and trunks

And memories stored on the wall

I am from Tennessee

Six Word Memoir

Evan

Ask me again in a month.

Julia

I am from the mountains
From Rockies and Appalachians
I am from bears that roam the secluded woods
Tall, dark, it smells like pines
I am from tulips, flowers with petals of deep purple
I'm from gardens with large onions and sour grapes
From Amy and Jay
I'm from a cabin in the ice cold Carolina air
From the large living room where we watch baseball
From the "You can do it" and the "Don't give up"
I'm from a Baptist Church, where the sign "Faith Promise"
hangs on the front door
I'm from Tennessee
Mountains and streams
From the father with the scarred eye from the car accident years
ago
From dusty pictures hanging on the walls
I am from Tennessee, a place that holds so much

What the Future Holds

Julia

Do you know what the future holds?
Do you know the life I'll live?
The things I'll give?
Do you know the places I'll go?
The people I'll know?
Do you know the things I'll see?
The person I'll be?
Do you know what I'll encounter in the next hour?
Do you know what the future holds?

Erica

I am from paperback books

From Snicket and Rowling

I am from Persian carpets, genuine, extravagant

They felt like magic

I'm from rhododendrons

And the lightning tree, broken and burned

From Red Sox games and heavy accents

From Dave and Renee and Julia

I am from well-mannered gossipers and ill-mannered oyster-
throwers

From cats landing on four feet and gold-plated track spikes

I am from confirmations and non-singing Catholics

I am from fields in Ireland

Fish and cheese

From the firefighters turned engineers and ever-changing hair
colors

I am from pictures behind the unstable wall in the unused garage

Always there, longing to be found

Haiku

Erica

Water runs clear swift

Pushing our limits of breath

Not stopping not here

Endless stacks shelves full

Silent adventures inside

Waiting to be read

Sydney

I am from Chacos

From Bath and Body Works and Nike

I am from flowers by doors, colorful and bold

They smell as beautiful as they look

I am from leaves on the trees and rose bushes with petals of pink and red

I'm from chicken and dumplings on Christmas

From Kasey and Greg and Cameron

I'm from short height and brown hair

And dimples in our cheeks

From "Treat others the way you want to be treated" and "Help others when they are in need"

I'm from Maryville Church of Christ

From Bible classes and Vacation Bible School

Sausage balls and banana pudding

From lake days, the park, and a teacher mom

I am from short height, camping trips, and lake days

I'm from Maryville, Tennessee

Haiku

Sydney

Fall leaves fall

Bring cold winter winds

Snow cover bare tree branches

Spring flowers

Petals everywhere

Cover the land with happiness

Meet

I am from PlayStation 3

From video games and food

I am from a very big house and

Nice and cool

It feels comfortable and safe

A good house

I am from the Tulsi, a Hindu religious plant

I'm from Indian temples

We go every year

I'm from the two main Indian Festivals

The Navratri and Diwali

I am from Kiran and Sejal and my sister, Shivani

Alexis

I am from tacos
From beef and pork
I am from camping
Warm tents that feel amazing
I am from flowers, daisies with yellow centers and white petals
I'm from family at Christmas
From Sabrina and David
Tall talkers
I from "Be nice to others" and "Be respectful"
I'm from the Lord and John 3:16
I'm from The University of Tennessee Medical Center
From sloppy-Joes and spaghetti
From the time my grandparents took me to the beach and we
found sand dollars
From going to Splash Country with my parents
I'm from Knoxville, Tennessee

Herchelene

I am from the rice fields

From avocados and noodles

I am from talkative, rambunctious, family etiquette

It felt delightful

I am from the sampaquita, the Philippine national flower

From the mango tree, sweet and juicy

I'm from Andre and Aileen

From cell phones and laptops

From a grateful and contented family

I'm from the glorious ruins, the blood that ran down His body

for our sins

I'm from the Northern Mariana Island

Pancit canton and pandesal (bread)

From the monkey bite on my mother's leg,

I am from the lover of Christ

A connoisseur of photo taking

Six Word Memoir

Herchelene

God's love came to my rescue.

Noah

I am from snares

From Yahama and innovations

I am from the hills next to the city

It could be loud, but at times peaceful

I am from valleys and the mountains, with their natural beauty

I am from dandelions and sunflowers, blowing and swaying in
the wind

I'm from backyard barbeques and green eyes

From David and Tammy and Zack

I'm from humor, positivity, and athletics

From "Give 110%" and "Never back down"

I'm from Jesus, who is the Son of God

I'm from Murfreesboro and Ireland

Chicken and spaghetti

From the exploded Monster drink

In a scrapbook spilling with years

I am from the beat of life

The amazingly awesome Noah

Hunter

I am from chocolate
From Hershey and 100 Grand
I am from kitchen cabinets, filled with all sorts of delicious food
Tidy, it tasted like mints
I am from apple trees and apples, red and delicious
I'm from Christmas Eve
And smart minds
From Charles and Linda and Makenzie
I'm from short tempers *and* patience
From Heaven and the military
I believe in God
I'm from San Diego, California, and Wrights
Pizza and chicken chili
From the walk home years ago with a dog following me
From the time my dad injured his leg playing baseball
From the family pictures in a fire-proof box in my home
I'm from a love of archery
I am from San Diego, California
I'm Hunter

Haiku

Hunter

In spring leaves grow
In fall the leaves fall freely
Always to be squashed

Five seven then five
Is the basis of haiku
Follow this guideline

Hannah

I am from the city
From loud noises and car beeps
I am from big city lights
With many people and many places
It sounded loud and looked bright
I am from trees, green and sticky, that turn different colors in fall
I'm from a party family
And my lookalike mother
From Lynn and Mack and Taylor
I'm from a chill family that does everything together
From Santa Claus and the Tooth Fairy
From "Believe that there is only one God" and "God is real"
From a military family and a great brother who is a junior in
high school
From my mom who was adopted
From family pictures at the lake, my brother always on the left
side
I always get the right side
I'm from peaceful lake-watching
I am from city lights

Samantha

From Apple and American Eagle
I am from rivers
Beautiful, wonderful
They taste like water
I am from the beauty of my mother
I'm from the deer of the woods
Brown and fluffy
I am from medicine that helps me
I am from turkey dinners and blue eyes
From Darcie and Robert and James
I am from hugs and kisses
From "Do what you want," and "Be happy"
I'm from Christianity, crosses
I'm from Alabama, watermelon and blueberries
From blonde hair and mountains
I am from allergies, pine trees, and Converse

I Remember When
Samantha

I remember that day when you first walked in
You made me test every relationship I had
Oh, you were so good, but, oh, so bad
I remember when you said you'd try
But really you only made me cry
I now look on that day and say
"Thank God I got away."

Personal Poem

Samantha

I'm just a girl

Who loves to be lazy

Someone who doesn't care about what I do

I just float through time

I may be a weird person, I may have a weird life

But I'm still the same as everyone else

Right?

I'm silly, crazy, all of the above

People call me too nice

I reply, "Really?"

And they just nod and go back to eating

I like rainy days when the sun doesn't shine

It's because I like the dark

My dad tells me to turn the lights on

I want to say no, but I very well do so

Average life, right?

I like what I like

Please do not judge

You like what you like

I will not judge

Maybe I am too nice

But that's just me

Charli

I am from dance
From iPhones and Chacos
I am from the warm, cozy, and classy house at the end of the
street
I am from rivers, spectacular and beautiful
I am from oak trees and daisies
I am from beautiful seedlings that sprout gloriously
From Christmas together and blonde hair
I am from Leslie and Michael and Sydney
I'm from annoying family time and being loud
From monsters and the Tooth Fairy
I'm from Christianity
I'm from Maryville
Cookies and fruit
From the time my father worked at the Bi-Lo and my mother
worked at a car dealership
I am from the park
I am from Maryville, Tennessee

Seth

I am from pencils

From Paper Mate

And fly racing

I am from the carpet under my bed, dark, quiet, it felt soft

I am from strawberry bushes and rose bushes, whose vines are

both prickly

I am from hunting and awesomeness

From Michael and Susan and Rex

I am from fishing and loudness

From being loved and being active

I'm from a Godly family

From Friendsville

Mac 'n cheese and bread

From killing a deer with my dad

I'm from tall stature and the park

I am from the loves of hunting, fishing, and riding dirt bikes

I am Seth

Memorable Moment

Seth

My most memorable moment is when I was 5 years old. I was in Virginia, and I'd just learned how to ride a bike. I was riding in around in a circle. When I went to turn, I was going too fast, and had to slam on the brakes to slow down. When I hit the brakes, I went over the handle bars, and landed on my face. My mouth was bursting out blood, and I cried. My mom says that I had blood all over me and she froze. My aunt suddenly picked me up, and gave me some pain killers. I fell asleep, and when I woke up I realized that I had lost all of my front teeth. My aunt later showed me the teeth she had to pull out of my mouth. Over the last couple of days even more teeth fell out.

And from this experience I learned that you need to slow down when going around turns.

Cade

I am from matches

From spray paint and skateboards

I am from the hay bales in the barn

Hot and sunny, it sounded of wind blowing through the trees

I am from the old silver maple tree, grey and tall

I'm from football games and hairy legs

From Bryan and Andrew

I'm from driving fast and breaking things

From "Working hard gets you far" and "Behave"

I'm from Christianity, from "Treat everyone as you treat
yourself"

From Virginia, Scotland and the Highland Games

Haggis and Shepard's Pie

From Crazy Uncle Joe exploding dynamite in the pond

From the kindness of Ruth

And the hallways

I am from the farm near the lake and the rolling hills of Scotland

Emily

I am from music
From Steinway and Fender
I'm from charcoal and wood, black, fiery, it smelled smoky and
warm
I am from the garden, pansies and sunflowers
The dirt and soil and brightness of them on a Sunday
I'm from coziness and love
From Kirsten and Rob and Nana Pat
I'm from jokes and laughs that made our stomachs ache
From "Not before dinner!" and "You have too many toys!"
I'm from Christians, from the Savior and Baptist churches
I'm from Knoxville, Tennessee
Cornbread and brownies
From Sunday meals with my dad and "cooking shows" we used
to put on
And playing piano with my grandmother
I am from these moments in time, from my special family tree
that never stops blooming,
Growing more and more each and every day

Six Word Motto

Emily

Music quite simply is beautiful emotion.

Leah

I am from hair spray
From Clinique and Hershey
I am from roses in the front lawn, pink and gentle, smelling
sweet
I am from blueberry bushes, small and fragile, a light shade of
purple
I'm from Saturday brunches and gag gifts on Christmas Eve
From Rebecca, Noah, Grant, and Steve
I'm from "germaphobes"
And lots and lots of hugs
From "Love and knowledge are key" and "God created our
family"
I'm from church, where God made everything, including you
and me
I'm from Knoxville and the "boonies"
Biscuits and gravy and cookies
From the people who fought *for* my country and the love shown
from my family
I explore the scrapbook filled with memories
From old wives' tales and "I love you"
I am from the worn picture Bible and frilly dresses
I'm from "The Old Rugged Cross"
Where I was forgiven from my sins

I'm from The University of Tennessee Hospital

Cake and chocolate gravy

From the first time my parents met and the countless times my

older brother prayed for a sister

I'm from my favorite picture; it sits on my nightstand

I am from the family that I love and more laughs still to come

Henley

I am from books

From Harry Potter and Percy Jackson

I am from the red-brick home on the end of Lisa Drive

Unique, different from the other houses, it smelled like cloves
and oranges

I am from the sun and the blooming cherry tree

Giving warmth on cool days and beauty during the spring

I'm from opening presents on Christmas and humor

From Blake, my dad, and Tonya, my mom, and everyone else in
my family

I'm from stubbornness and sarcasm

From "Patience is a virtue" and "Don't be mean to your little
siblings"

I'm from "Jesus loves me, this I know"

From craft time in children's church

I'm from Knoxville and France

French fries Beignets and

From making snowmen and sledding down hills with my
younger siblings

And putting a hat and pink ears on my little sister's golden head

From helping my little brother climb trees without breaking his
bones

From the picture albums in the china cabinet

I am from people who love and moments that matter

"Lemonade"

Henley

Warm sunlight

Cloudless sky

Wooden table on the side of the road

Handmade sign and

A jar that says "tips"

Cooler under the little tablecloth

Patiently waiting

Tempted to try some

Postman gets a glass and gives us our mail

Hours later

Sticky fingers

No lemonade is left

But the memories remain

Megan

I am from wild horses
From bubblegum and poetry
I am from the brick house in the city, large, warm, it felt inviting
and forgiving
From oak trees and the daisies, quiet yet attentive
I'm from family dinners and intelligence
From Carol and Scott and humanitarians
I'm from the OCD cleaners, the opinionated and outspoken
From "Follow even the craziest of dreams" and "Don't let
anyone silence your voice"
I'm from Christians, those that believe everything happens for a
reason
I'm from Atlanta
From German chocolate cake and cupcakes
From the kid that threw a baseball through the window and the
ballerina
From a hat box under the bed overflowing with family photos
Memories long ago forgotten but stored in my heart
I am from never regretting, using every opportunity, and being
able to look back on life with a smile and laughter

Aaron

I am from books

From shooting basketball hoops, hiking and biking

I'm from my cozy house in Maryville

The Smoky Mountains and the Himalayas

I am from family reunions and blue-green eyes

From my mom, Rebecca, and my dad, Daniel

I am from Klingensmiths, Klenks, Striplings, and Olsons

From being told I was going to India and being told I could go to
boarding school there

I am from acceptance of different cultures and religions

I'm from Knoxville, Tennessee

And ancestors from Germany, England, and Sweden

Spaghetti and Indian food

I'm from mom, growing up in upstate New York and going to
India seven times

From dad, growing up in West Virginia and going to Harvard

And where my parents met in Madison, Wisconsin

I am from one grandparents' house in Beckley, West Virginia,
and another in Denver, Colorado

I am from kindness and worldliness

Six Word Motto

Aaron

Some things go well. Others, badly.

Marissa

I am from Mason jars
From picnic tables and lemonade
I am from cat hair on the carpet, white and fluffy
I am from bougainvillea, the ocean, and the rustle of leaves in
the fall
I am from spring break trips and curiosity
From Kyle, Grandma, and Grandpa
I am from warm vacations
From "Never give up" and "Clean your room!"
I am from Christian faith and praying before dinner
I am from Fort Sanders Hospital
From blueberries, tea, and spaghetti
I am from Grandpa, who is always ahead of his time
And animal lovers
With our pictures on the wall for display
I am from Maryville, where we have barbecues and football
games

Lauren

I am from glistening sandy beaches
From sunscreen and Computers L.T.D.
I am from sweet smelling and rowdy, sisters that don't count
I am from sounds like New York happy time
I am from a rose garden and the oak tree growing tall
Beautiful, rough, yet limber when handled
I'm from Christmas tree parties and hazel eyes
From mother and father and sister
I'm from partiers and early risers
From "Drizzles are toilet water from a plane"
And "If you were born with a veil of skin over your face, you are
special"
I'm from the heart of God, with a side of Jesus in there
Spaghetti and pepper and bread
From the bursting my finger open with a weight of my brothers
The short but loud
I am from the hallway that drags on
I am from those who care

Kip

I am from computers

From Apple and Lego

I am from the beautiful home that is made of purple

From the house that was colored like the flame of a dragon

I am from the green tree and the flower with orange leaves

I'm from Christmas and treats

From Jen and Chris and Jimmy

I'm from typical loud yelling and really loud food chomping

From Santa Claus and the Easter bunny

I'm from Christianity

From God lovers

I'm from Chicago

Pizza and hot dogs

From long noses

I am from great music lovers

A Six Word Memoir
Kip

Knock, knock.
Who's there?
I AM.

Elizabeth

I am from bobby pins

From Tide and hairspray

I am from brick and gardens alongside the deck, open, inviting

It feels like where I belong

I am from the pines and the rocks in the riverbed

Smooth and pretty

I'm from Christmas gatherings and dark features

From Diana and Jenny and Joe

I'm from cooking at home and playing music

From "Believe in yourself" and "We love you "

I'm from Christianity, believing in the one true God

I'm from Augusta, Georgia,

Tacos and salsa

From the people who poke out other people's eyes with light
sabers

From musicians who can play anything

I'm from pictures in the album in the bookcase

I am from dancing and playing music in the Deep South

Brandy

I am from sweet tea

From mud fights and late nights

I am from large families with traditions and loud cousins

It feels warm and hearty, with jokes and pranks that keep you on your toes

I am from the majestic oak trees that were as tall as the sky, and racing to the top to watch the distance cars drive by

I am from gathering together and having a feast

From the smart and debating family

I am from Kim and Jason, my loving parents, and Grandma Teresa and Grandpa Roy

I am from laid back conversations and continuous laughing

I'm from "Respect your elders" and "If you can't say something nice, don't say anything at all"

I am from praying every day

And thanking God for everything I have

From knowing that God always has a plan

I'm from Orlando Florida

Hot days, oranges, and mockingbirds

I am from clumsy family members, who stand on office chairs with wheels to hang decorations

From my Aunt Niki's breaking her arm right before her wedding

I am from my Aunt Trish melting corn on the cob holders in the oven on our Thanksgiving ham

I am from stacks of photo albums piled in the closets

I am from a workaholic family who try their hardest to make everyone happy

I am from a strong family who would do anything for each other

Sam

I am from grass

From Clorox and Gap

I'm from the house of adventure and fun

Warm and familiar, it tasted sweet

I am from water, flowing with new rains

I'm from gathering and eyes from Beth and Jason and Walt

I'm from creators and doers

From Santa Claus and the Tooth Fairy

I'm from the church with art on Sundays

I'm from East Tennessee

Apple pie and eggs

From small feet, brown hair

From memories stored in the living room

I'm from these times

When I was young and the trees were full of adventure

Shivani

I am from the pink bicycle on the front porch
From the bananas lying on the dinner table and the television in
the living room
I am from a two story house that is always kept, clean, sparkling,
it looked like a brand new car
I am from apple trees in the backyard and the evergreen tree
whose greenery never budges
I'm from candy and cameras
From Mahesh and Shilpa
I'm from stubborn and boisterous laughter
From being told that my mom can see everything I do at school
each minute and that different acronyms stood for totally
different things than the originals
I'm from being punished for doing something wrong because He
is watching me
From remembering songs
I'm from Toronto, and the orange, white and green Indian flag
From Curry and Naan
From the disease that my Grandfather died fighting
From the numerous photos taken by my father
From my closet, a shelf trickling with old memories
I am from the moments when we moved three places and the
faint smell of candles

Six Word Motto

Shivani

Live like it's your last day.

Isaiah

I am from State Farm

From Nike and American Eagle

I am from Chucky Cheese

"Where a kid can be a kid!"

It tasted cheesy, extraordinary and felt kid-tastic, like a dream

I am from sneezewort yarrow and the monkey puzzle tree

Whirling wind

I'm from Xbox

From being outgoing

From Randall and Tee and Randi

I'm from the coolest, the most awesome

The fantastic

From "Treat others the way you want to be treated" and

"Faith, family, football"

I'm from Baptists in Tennessee

Mac-n-cheese and sweet tea

From the time Tee ran into a window

I'm from the pictures, along EVERY wall in my house

Memories

I am a six-foot lean, mean, machine

Culton

I am from orange Jell-O

From valleys, depths, and shallows

I am from flowing rivers, loud and running with pride

They taste sweet and bitter

I am from the orange tree, the sprout to success

I am from Mexican food on Easter

From Rob and Rob and Dorothy

I'm from the loud and crazy family

From the rich Tennessee valley and the winning Tennessee

Volunteers

I'm from the Methodist church

From trying not to drift and trying to stay on the right path

I'm from the hills of the Tennessee Valley

Steak and barbecue

From the house of two teachers in a family of engineers

Pictures in books, on the shelf collecting dust

I am from a rich Tennessee heritage

Kasey

I am from steep hills

From honeysuckle and small pawn shops

I am from a tiny, hidden town

I'm from The Great Smoky Mountains

And big soccer fields

I am from family that goes to a small beautiful park every year

From Kathryn and Andrew and the Grizzells

And big blue eyes

I am from television on the porch and modern warfare games

From "Holding your horses" and "Silly goose"

I'm from Jesus Christ, the son of God

Who saved me from my sins

From Knoxville, Tennessee and Spanish influence

Pudding and biscuits

From the time my mom went into the pool with her phone in her
pocket

I'm from the time my dad almost drove from church without
making sure I was in the car first

Memories in a box

I'm from Tennessee, Seymour, where a small town makes a big
difference

Jenna

I am from glasses
From Nike shorts and Chacos
I am from the house on the hill, stone-covered, unique, it looked
like a castle
I am from a dog named after rose petals and frog-shaped flower
pots
I'm from Cedar Point and dark curly hair
From Maria and Andrew
From Gram and Papa
I'm from six-foot-tall cousins and bad eyes
From "Please" and "Thank you"
I'm from Christianity, prayers before dinner
I'm from Florida, Ireland, Germany, and Lebanon
Baked chicken and mashed potatoes
From Grandfather, who can't stop dancing once he starts
And cousins who are taller than I am
From old pictures in scrapbooks
I am from Tennessee and Florida, friends and family, dogs not
cats, love not hate, positive not negative, "Always be happy" and
"You're not fully dressed without a smile!"

Seth

I am from running shoes
From Altras and Adidas
I am from an old neighborhood, the confined space that felt so
full yet never cramped
I am from butterfly bushes and Bradford pears, whose berries
popped when I threw them
I'm from bike rides and sports
From Julie and Dick
I'm from stubborn politeness and lengthy explanations
From "You have potential," and "Form your own ideas"
I'm from a God of morals, who stands for what is right
I am from spirituality
I'm from the North, but born in Tennessee
Buttered corn and soybeans
From an engineer who built motherboards for warheads
And a mother who runs the Boston Marathon
On the dusty shelves lay the organized photos, holding both joy
and tragedy
They sometimes seem like light-years away
I am from a blessed life, where I am learning from my mistakes
and the experiences of others
I am from making the most of every opportunity and respecting
those who love me

Haiku

Seth

Maryville, my school
Education and effort
Prepare me for life

Education, I
I try hard to succeed
I will be proud soon

Reese

I am from soccer balls at nice sports complexes
From Nike and Adidas
I am from a home with lots of bathrooms and warm cozy beds
I am from flowers, white roses that lay on caskets
I am from shooting guns at the farm and playing sports in the
backyard
I am from thumb sucking 'til 9 years old and video games all my
life
From "Always do your best at everything" and "Always work
hard no matter what"
I am from Christianity, church on Sundays and Wednesdays
And any other time you can be there
I'm from Greenville, South Carolina
Creamed corn on Easter and special sauce during the summer
From my brothers breaking bones
The leg at a soccer game
I'm from my father's heart surgery
I'm from my grandfather's lake
I am from the hearth of my living room

Six Word Memoir

Reese

Mcgregor Douglas Allen, The Mac Foundation.

Courtney

I am from pointe shoes
From Capezio and Bloch
I'm from a loving home, warm and friendly, it feels cozy
I am from a pincushion flower, the light purple color
I'm from big dinners on Thanksgiving and brown eyes
From Dawn and Chris, and James
I'm from biting tongues and making up songs
From "Don't play outside by yourself" and "Don't run up and
down the stairs"
I'm from Christianity and baptisms
From Maryville, Tennessee
Corn and mashed potatoes on holidays
From riding tubes down the river, my lively and funny sister, the
crazy and loud cousin
From taking pictures in front of the Christmas tree
I am from the Greenbelt that runs through my backyard
From walking and playing games

Six Word Motto

Courtney

Dance is pure movement of emotion.

Alexis

I am from a glass of homemade sweet tea
From the lemon on the side and the ice cubes in the glass
I am from a table that holds glass to the floor, it sounds like
thunder
I am from grass and sky
From a pencil on the desk and the driver of a car
From Scottie in Heaven and the light from up above
I'm from wheels on cars, glass you look through, and
headphones you listen to
From trash in the trash can and keys in the ignition
I'm from a bell on top of a church and a note in the church
hymnal
I'm from Knoxville, towers in the sky
From the fish in the water and the pizza on the table
From the story of the girl named "Ash-lee" with the weird name
spelled "Lee" and not "Ley"

Allyson

I am from love

From Mom and Dad

I am from the small home, filled with children

I am from the plant of people, the old plant of life

I am from blue eyes

Diana and Alan

I am from loud and loving

From "Be yourself" and "Dream big"

I am from Christians, a Jesus-loving family

I am from Tennessee

Ham and potatoes

I am from long hair, small height, and blue eyes

From the pictures in my house that appeared before I blinked

I am from a mountain heritage, family get-togethers

I'm from family who cares for one another

Amanda

I am from a backpack
From a book and a binder
I am from spider webs in the bushes
From rose bushes and oak trees
I am from Canada and Italy
From Ann and James and Jolene
I am from talkers and stubborn thinkers
From being able to fly and being a super hero
I am from Baptists
From the mountains of Maryville, Tennessee
Lasagna and deviled eggs
From awkward conversations, the sharing of favorite songs, and
cherishing every moment we are together
I am from pictures in boxes in the back of dark closets
I am a girl who is generally happy and caring, who lives in the
mountains of Tennessee and enjoys listening to music

Aric

I am from pencils

From iPods and Xbox One

I am from the grass under the old oak tree

Cool, crisp, it tasted like summer

I am from the old oak tree, tall and wispy

I'm from an old red barn and athletes

From Derek and Esther and Alyssa

I'm from jokers and loudmouths

From "Don't play with your food" and "Don't point with that finger"

I'm from Bethlehem and the empty tomb

I'm from Germany

And Lisa

From the pond out back, where if you aren't careful, you will be "swimming with the fishes"

I'm from the place to laugh and play

From pictures on the bookshelf and pictures on the walls

You will probably have a harder time trying not to see them than trying to see them

I am from smoke and steam

Haiku

Aric

I am happy when
You give me lots of cookies
I like that a lot

Football is always
Going on no matter what
I love it so much

Austin

I am from video games
From Halo Reach and Halo 4
I am from a three story house with two bedrooms
Small, full, tan in color
I am from nature, the iris, a blue with a hint of purple
From visiting Virginia
From green eyes
From my Grandpa, and Grandpa Tom, and Tom, Jennifer and
Dennis
I'm from the Thomas family and kind hearts
From "You can become whatever you want to be" and "You will
be intelligent"
I'm from in between, not leaning toward one side or the other
I believe that there may have been someone like Jesus, but he
doesn't have these other worldly powers that people think he has
I'm from mom's ancestors from Mexico and dad's ancestors
from Ireland
Enchiladas and potatoes
From family pictures saved onto various flash drives
I am Austin

"Rebel Haiku"

Austin

Determined, strong hearted, talented

Always doing the best possible

And will always win

Letter to Future Self

Emily

Dear Future Emily,

    Hey, so you're older now. That's really great that you made it this far. I'm here just to ask a few questions but also to see how you are doing. Since I *am* you, I know exactly what you wanted to accomplish, so here I am in 9th grade tech class, writing you a letter that you'll probably never read again.

    First of all, I want to know something simple. How are you? Are you okay? Is everything working out like you planned all those years ago? I hope so; you had big dreams, and I sincerely hope you achieved them and that you continue to shoot for the stars. Did you ever go out of state to college? I hope so; I know how much you wanted to get away. You wanted to start fresh and live a new life. I wonder if you changed your name; you never liked the name "Emily" and wanted it to be something more unique.

    When you were younger all you wanted to do was go to New York. Are you there now? Or, do you plan to go there soon? Maybe you've been there already and moved on to better things. I hope you got into NYU; I know how much that would mean to you. If you are in New York, did you get that loft apartment for which you saved for so long? If you are there now,

262

I hope you are with someone you actually like to be around. Maybe the idea of an apartment with Rebecca worked out? Or maybe not. I guess I'll just wait and see. Speaking of New York, did you pursue acting? I'm sure you still love it. I hope you at least tried because I know it was always your dream. Maybe you just bailed out and became a teacher. I hope you try to do something even greater if that doesn't go anywhere.

One more thing; do you travel? I know how much you wanted to. You wanted to go everywhere: Germany, Ireland, Paris, England, Holland, or maybe even Scotland. Oh boy, do I hope you travel! I hope you see all the sights meet and all the people. Maybe you've finally met someone? If not, that's fine; you have your whole life ahead of you. I just hope you don't get your heart broken.

Anyway, I should probably get going. I hope you are okay. Just be yourself and let life come to you. I hope you're doing wonderfully, or at least better than you are now. Stay Safe.

Sincerely,
15-year-old Emily

"Fantasy Football"

Nathan

My team is good enough to get me 0 and 3.

Can I get my best running back healthy again?

Please?

I need to win games.

I must.

A playoff appearance is all I lust.

Would it even *be* a Super Bowl without me?

I need 30 points from Matt Ryan.

And a couple TD catches from Dez Bryant.

Rashad Jennings can't fumble.

Alfred Morris don't be too humble.

I need Jamaal Charles to be a football tyrant.

Cayden

I am from the mockingbird state

From Nike and American Eagle

I am from black and red Rebels

I am from purple irises and the Smoky Mountains

I am from wakeboarding and wavy hair

From James and Misty and Diane

I'm from big spenders and competitors

From "Be careful! Don't touch that!" and "Have fun!"

I'm from Faith Promise Church, from Maryville, Tennessee

Starbucks and chicken

From the Jet Ski my dad drove up the bank on the Fontana

camping trip

From memories stored in the top of the closet

I am from high-maintenance, loving, and caring friends that get

hyped up for Rebel football

Fight Song/Chant Dedicated to Coach Upton

Jacob

Coach Upton you're so fine,

You're so fine you blow my mind,

COACH UPTON!

(audience) HEY, HEY

COACH UPTON!

(audience) HEY, HEY, HEY!!!

WE CAN'T SEE YOU!

(CLAP, CLAP……….CLAP, CLAP, CLAP)

GET ON THE SCOREBOARD!

WE CAN'T SEE YOU!

(CLAP, CLAP……….CLAP, CLAP, CLAP)

GET ON THE SCOREBOARD!

Braden

I am from boxers in the dryer

From Hollister and American Eagle

I am from the three story house on that one street

The big red house, it looks like two stories

I am from raw metal from the ground

Metal, for making swords

I am from staying at the house for Christmas every year

From the athletic and smart

From Clarence and Amy and Katie

I am from courage and honesty

From "You are strong" and "You are smart"

I'm from a Baptist family, from strong beliefs in God and

knowing He's the one who saved us from our sins

I'm from Murfreesboro, Tennessee

From Grandmama and Grandpapa

From macaroni and brownies

From a dramatic family with a complaining sister and mother

I'm from a dad who is always laid back and cool, but hard

working, not lazy

From family pictures in an old book, hidden in a drawer covered

by dust

I am from the stereotypical southeast, where some people "talks

real slow" and "ain't too bright"

Fight Song for Maryville Rebels

Braden

We are the Maryville Rebels and we win, win, win!

We are the Maryville Rebels and we fight, fight, fight!

We are the Rebels and we are the best!

Six Word Memoir

Braden

<u>Hannah Strange is so fantastically gorgeous!!!</u>

Limericks by Robin

I'd better screw it back on
I won't leave it off for long
He can't see the rain
He can't feel pain
Probably because his head is gone

Autumn seems to be a downer
Leaves dried, and all the wilted flowers
But what they forget
All that they left
Back at the end of summer

I'll scream through all my hate
Even though it's about to break
I shouldn't cry
My mom tells me why
It really sucks to be constipated

The array of emotions that I get
When I'm reminded of that bet
It turns me brown
When I remember how

I tripped the syringe-carrying vet

Hallie

I am from Jolly Ranchers
From Nike and Purel
I am from pictures on the wall, hanging, lovely
It always felt so cozy
I am from aloe plants in the kitchen
I'm from the mole holes in the backyard that ruined the scenery
I am from holding hands and praying on Thanksgiving
From curly hair and freckles
I am from Jonda and others
From leaving my socks in my shoes
I'm from forgetting to put the twist tie on the bread
That's where I'm from

Six Word Memoir

Hallie

Tripped on mistakes, tumbled on reality.

Jared

I am from soccer fields
From FIFA
I am from indoors and outdoors
Hot and cold
It sounded like something bouncing
I am from tomato plants, red and tall
I'm from Thanksgiving Dinner
From Steve and Colby and Jeremy
And tallness in stature
I'm from the tendency to yell
From "Don't trust the man in the big black van" and "Money
doesn't buy happiness"
I'm from the cross, Christianity
I'm from Knoxville, Tennessee, and the Great Smoky Mountains
Baked beans and corn bread
From the family vacation when my brother made funny faces
and I laughed at him
And Sandy Springs Park
I am a guy who loves humor

Jacob

I am from shoulder pads and knee pads

From dirt and mud under cleats

I am from blood and sweat on our uniforms

And black paint on our faces

I'm from tears of joy and tears of pain

From the weak to the strong

And what lies ahead of us is a mystery and only God can tell us

what path to go on

Under my bed is a box spilling old football pictures of my dad

I want to keep our generation going on

I'm from "If you have a dream don't let go of it" and

"Don't stop believing in yourself" and

"Do not let your dreams disappear"

I am from knowing that someday God will give me a sign

And a future

Katie

I am from ballet
From Apple and Nike
I am from a house with a white picket fence, it looked as white
as paper with little points
It tasted like newly fallen snow
I am from holly bushes and the maple tree, whose big green
leaves surround me like a blanket
I'm from the Maine log cabin and pale skin
From Robert and Darcy and Ozzie and Kelly
I'm from wittiness and stubbornness and tradition
From "Don't lie" and "Clean up after yourself" and
"Do your best"
I'm from small white churches with liberal Christian beliefs
I'm from East Tennessee, warm southern hospitality
Homemade apple pie and mashed potatoes with gravy
From my grandmother's train rides to visit a handsome soldier
And a 92-year-old great-grandfather who went skydiving
I am from pictures in the dust filled cabinet above the desk
I am from the Maine woods and sunny California
I am strong, driven, ambitious, traditional, and adventurous

Haiku

Katie

Leaving their home bare
Orange and gold leaves fall silently
Flying off into the sky

Snow blinds the eye with a glisten
Reflecting the sun ever so slightly
Melting slowly till spring

Kevin

I am from kitchen tables
From Windex and Kellogg's
I am from a brick building, poured concrete walls with an awful
cell signal
It tastes salty
I am from Venus fly traps, the carnivorous ones, I eat everything
I'm from "Go clean your room" and "Do it or else"
From Mum and Dad
And that one pet fish I had that died in 3 days
Its name was Whale
I'm from "Kid, go clean stuff" and "But when you're done, go
play something"
"Maybe an instrument or two"
From "equal opportunity" and "not equal outcome"
I'm from Christ, First Baptist Church of Maryville
I'm from Florida and Ohio
Hungary and Germany
Britain and Scotland
Scottish food
From the time I accidentally got locked in the basement
I am from Tennessee, the mountains

"Little Me"
Lexi

I'd tell you to be brave
To be prepared for life now
I'd tell you things aren't as
Easy as they seem
I'd tell you to never give up
Also to keep your head up
To be prepared for bullies,
Hard work, losing friends,
And making new friends
I'd tell you to never worry about
What people think of you
Because it doesn't matter
Last I would tell you to
Smile more

Lexi

I am from shoes
From Vans and Doc Martens
I am from leaves lying on the ground, it smelled like cinnamon,
Warm and cozy
I am from trees that sway back and forth like they're dancing
I am from cheering and war fighting
From Rick and Traci
I'm from the talkative world and fun land
From the world of monsters under my bed and people telling me
not to worry about being judged
I'm from church with friends then and church with my own
family now
I'm from cold but bright lights of a small room and places all
around the world
Apple pies and home cooked meals
From falling off a scooter and breaking my arm and my sister
cutting her finger trying to peel me an orange
I' from spending time in the woods
I am from stages I sing on without feeling nervous

Shania

I am from socks

From Dawn and Finish

I am from the house, little and cozy, cream-colored and boring

It felt smooth like a leather couch

I am from flowers, daisies

Dancing in the wind as if they were me

I'm from caring yet obnoxious

From Brian and Sheri and Bryson

I'm from judgmental and talkative

From "Boys have cooties" and "Boys are trouble"

I'm from Maryville, Tennessee

Pizza and chicken nuggets

From falling off a metal roof and cutting my toe

To falling in love with Justin Bieber, the "Teen Heart Throb"

I am from dancing like nobody is there and only worrying about

the present

Six Word Motto
Ali

Never let the world transform you.

Kaitlyn

I am from the Smoky Mountains
From Cherry Coke and Cherry Pepsi
I am from a sweet, loving, caring family home, nice, happy
It felt nice and cuddly and soft, like fur
I am from animals, cats
And lilies, sweet, purple and white
I'm from family time and competitive
From MoonPies and Summer and Rock Star
I'm from a lovable family, talkative and fun
From "Treat your elders with respect and you will receive
respect back"
And "Do unto others as you would have them do unto you"
I'm from the cross that Jesus died on
God is the Father, Son, and the Holy Spirit
He created Earth and everything living on it
I'm from Maryville, Tennessee

Tian

I am from China

From a huge city and the long side beach

I am from an ocean by the beach

Where crabs live and people swim, it tastes salty

I'm from New Year celebrations and fireworks

From Wus and Chans And Zhens

I'm from the special foot and New Year reds

From "Keep good manners" and "Keep secrets for avoiding

trouble"

I'm from Buddhism, faith and believe in God

I'm from Fuzhou, China

Noodles and fresh cooked lobsters

From a Dad who is a chief and a great cook

And Mom who is a saleswoman

I'm from Dad, Mom and grandparents

I am from the world's longest history of a human country and

the world's most complicated language

Hashtags

Tian

I love to play #soccer,

My position in soccer is a #midfielder.

It is the most important position in the #team,

We protect our goal and score against the #enemy!

Spencer

I am from candy

From Snickers, a delicious chocolate caramel mixture

I'm from dirt under the back porch, above my cat

I am from blueberry bushes

Whose long-gone limbs I remember as if they were my own

I'm from fudge and chocolate, coco beans and sugar

I'm from my mother's womb

From dinosaur-shaped chicken nuggets (not actual dinosaurs or real chicken)

From the dead rabbit that my cat ate one evening

And the kitchen where we found my dog had been hit by a car and survived

I am from the vet telling us he was fine and giving me a Popsicle

Six Word Memoir

Spencer

What is that giraffe doing there?

Kate

I am from Clorox Bleach and Tic Tacs

I am from a plastic house with broken walls

It sounded like shrieking baboons

I am from cherry blossoms and watermelons

Beautiful, blossoming, and full of sweet juices

I'm from joking around and never being serious

From Judy and James and the great-grandparents

I'm from short tempers and fake smiles

From hopes of staying together and being a big happy family

I'm from blind faith and having something to believe in

I'm from North Carolina

Spicy noodles and schnitzels

From the German gun pointed at my Granddad's face

And the sticks and stones used to build my Grandma's house

From family photos at the zoo and the falls

I am from fallen tears that I kept to myself, but ended up using to

help nourish a beautiful flower that would become who I am

Haiku

Kate

Autumn is coming
The leaves are starting to fall
Jump into the leaves

It's getting colder
Sweater weather is coming
Time to bundle up

Mayuki

I am from a pencil case
From a ruler and a Sharpie
I am from the space underneath the legs of the desk
Narrow, lonely
I am from carnations, lavender, whose smell give me comfort
I'm from Christmas trees and contact lenses
From Miyako and Junkichi
I'm from the "No shoes inside the house" and
"Eat with chopsticks"
From fluffy dresses and piano practice
I'm from appreciation, because every bit of life is a miracle
I'm from Japan
Sushi and yakiniku
From the severe father who disciplined my grandmother with
strength and tenderness
And the big-hearted grandfather, who grows tons of fresh fruits
and vegetables in his garden
From the house of a peaceful village
I am who I am

Macie

I am from food
From Chick-fil-a and Rita's
I am from beaches, beautiful and sandy
They feel warm and breezy
I am from daisies, bright yellow
They smell amazing
I am from a party family
We always have a grand time
From Tyler and Trevor and David
I am from the fun and photogenic
From Santa Claus and the Tooth Fairy
I am from God, a strong believing Christian who follows ten
simple rules
I am from Maryville, Tennessee
Chicken and potatoes
From beaches and late night walks
Always going on vacation and going crab hunting late at night
The loving lady
I'm from pictures in my forever long closet filled with toys
I am from a small town twenty minutes away from the big city

Six Word Motto

Coleman

Nothing is worse than underperforming yourself.

Lauren

I am from baked goods
From Dollywood candy and Clorox wipes
I am from rocks in the backyard, gray-like, rough, looking like a maze
I am from pink lilies and dogwood trees with orange, luscious leaves
 I'm from holiday celebrations and freckles
From Tony, Michelle, and Whitney
I'm from the dependent and the reserved, from "Never give up" and "Be kind"
I'm from modern Baptists and the church in the city
I'm from southern Tennessee
Home-made bread and warm fudge
From my grandmother's everyday home-cooked meals and my grandfather's hard factory work
The wall above the dresser is full of old pictures that I will remember for eternity
I am from a close-knit family, a small and kind town, and memories that will last forever

Jasmine

I am from a city untamed

From charm bracelets and Bottle Cap Jewelry

I am from the small town of Maryville

I'm from oak trees and marvelous fields of jasmine

I am from football and blonde hair

From Carol and John

I am from the greatest family I could ever have

From, "Timeout" and "Go play outside"

I am from Christianity, from "Always love and cherish Jesus Christ"

I'm from Maryville

Spaghetti & meatballs and steak

From parents and grandparents, wonderful aunts and uncles, and best cousins ever

I am from pianos and singing

I am from love

Callie

I am from fuzzy socks

From Netflix and Anytizers chicken nuggets

I am from the cove of my neighborhood, smooth, friendly, it
sounded like laughter

I am from roses, the prickly flower, blood red and beautiful

I'm from lemon cake and brown hair

From Christy and Cory and Susan

I'm from procrastinators and the passionate

From "Love your enemies" and "Take up for yourself"

I'm from my God's not dead, He is coming back soon!

I'm from Jackson, in West Tennessee

Fried chicken and cornbread

From houses we've moved to because of my Dad's job and the
laughter of my Mamaw

In a scrapbook many smiling faces stare up at me

I am from a chubby phase as a child, an angry phase as a pre-
teen, and learning about life one mistake at a time

Jasmine

I am from a home
From "Tom and Jerry" and "Kim Possible"
I am from a big back yard
Bright green and full of birds, it looked beautiful
I am from rose bushes, pink, white, and red
From family game nights and movie nights
From Alissa and John and Michael
I am from movies every Saturday and staying up late on the
weekends
From "Eat your vegetables" and "Don't drink coffee or it will
stunt your growth"
I'm from praying before you eat and going to church every
Sunday
I'm from Tennessee
Chicken and potatoes
From my uncle holding me on his shoulders and my Pepere
babysitting me
From scrapbooks with great pictures
I am from all the nuts on the family tree

Zachary

I am from good music
From Dr. Pepper and Hot Pockets
I am from a vacation house, cozy, fun, it feels like home
I am from grass that your mom has asked you thousands of times
to cut
The really, really ugly grass that has been dying for weeks
I'm from looking at Christmas lights by force and warm hugs
From Michael and Niki and Mark
I'm from always eating dinner together because that's what good
families do
And watching television
From "Always eat your vegetables" and "Your room looks like a
refugee camp"
I'm from being able to believe whatever you want and not being
judged for it
I'm from Rocky Top
Where nothing beats mashed potatoes and more mashed potatoes
(we love mashed potatoes)
I'm from losing my dad at a young age and having a mom that
was always there
I am from good taste and hospitality, acceptance and love

Chase

I am from Maryville, Tennessee

From chili, corndogs, and "bob sandwiches"

I am from a regular home with two stories

It tasted like fried potatoes

I am from plants so I can grow

I am a tree, from the picnic and the backwoods

From CJ and Carson and Heather

I'm from family that loves to read books and have family outings

From Christian churches and "Don't be mean"

I'm from Christian churches, believers

I'm from Tennessee

Bacon and biscuits

From the cousin that jumped of the roof of our house

And the great-grandfather that died in a war

I'm from family pictures in a box in the living room

Hashtag Poem

Katelyn

#RosesAreRed

#VioletsAreBlue

#ILove#TacoBell

#AndNotYou

Courtney

I am from Yankees
From Whiteout and Apple
I am from the "Zoo"
Loud and fun, it smells like wet dog
I am from lily pads and frogs, slimy and wet
I'm from instruments and freckles
From Heidi and Chris and Harley
I'm from sleeping in class and having adventures
From Santa and the Easter bunny
I'm from lack of church visits and grilled chicken Sunday
I'm from New York
Irish soda bread and pretzels
From the fall off the incomplete porch and blonde moments
The hidden family pictures
I am from the house where everything is fun

Mason

I am from hay bales my father baled

From cattle and John Deere tractors

I'm from the woods that surround the house

I am from the oak my relatives cut down to keep them warm, I

felt the pain of the tree when it crashed into the ground

I am from hamburgers and Ford trucks, ducks and deer

I am from hard workers and over timers

From tough love and soft hearts

I'm from "He leadeth me beside still waters" in an old King

James Version Bible

From the Ten Commandments that I follow

I am from Strawberry Plains and the Holston River

Fried okra and sweet tea

From my father's hunting dog, Mac, and my mother's

perseverance through tough times

From a scrapbook where pictures remain from the era before me

A reminder of who I am and where I come from

I am from the moments my family had before me

Samuel

I am from my mom
From sand and Nerf guns
I am from a big, cozy, home
From a tree, the ocean
I am from visiting and coolness
From Kevin and Carolyn and Kilpatrick
I am from boredom and excitement
From "Don't put your bologna on your forehead" and
"Don't sword fight with your sister's crutches"
I am from Christianity
I'm from Oklahoma
Mac 'n cheese and bacon
From playing putt-putt and pool
And turkeys
I am from computer pictures of my childhood

Alex

I am from gun powder
From Duct tape and Glade
I am from white walls, slate roof and green grass, sour green
I'm from honey, the golden syrup
I am from the Lake House and blue eyes
From George and Jan and Robert
I'm from deadly stares and the happy smiles
From "Shut up" and "Sit down"
I'm from Baptists, Godly people
I'm from Tennessee and Canada
Chicken hearts and white hair
I'm from bald heads and pictures in a trunk
I am from gun powder and golden syrup

Dakotah

I am from a computer

From Xbox and PS3

I am from a house that my family has lived in for ages

A mess that is loved and hated at the same time

It looks like it has been vacant for years

I am from the tree in the back yard, it just sits there and is
boring, but start climbing and it becomes fun

I'm from family reunions every year and brown eyes

From Shannon and John and Michael

I'm from yelling at the games I play and jumping every time I
get excited

From "Don't touch that" and "Put it back"

I'm from staying at home and doing nothing on Sundays and
Wednesdays

I'm from my mom and Tennessee

Peanut butter fudge and peach pie

From a family of baseball players and one football player, and
my mom who works as a nurse

"A Baseball Poem"

Dakota

Baseballs are round

And so is the moon

So hit a homerun

Because this is for you

"One, two, three strikes you're out "

Ball four, walk and don't talk

When the game's over, show some respect

To the team that loses the old ball game

Sarah

I am from sweet tea
From Mayfield and Pals
I am from bricks on my house, brown and tan
I am from dandelions, big and yellow
From trees in my back yard, big and shady
I am from *Friday Night Lights* and football lovers
From Jeff and Shannon and Chris
I'm from church on Sundays and lunch after church
From the Tooth Fairy and Santa Claus
I am from Christianity and Virginia
From homemade ice cream and green beans
From the balloon my dad swallowed and the head my mom
cracked open
And Mamaw's house up on the hill
I am from big oak trees where family pictures are taken
I am from Virginia, and I am proud

Tristan

I am from a very dusty computer
From AMD and Nvidia
I am from yellow and brick, loud and alive, it looked clean
sometimes
I am from the tsubaki I guess, the flower that grows and dies
with no fragrance
I am from the white elephant and sarcasm
From Ben, Ben, and Bill
I'm from sarcasm spouted by me and my dad, and yelling
From "I was adopted" to "Sharing is caring"
I'm from science and more science
I'm from Knoxville, Tennessee
Pineapples and coconuts
From the time I smashed my finger in a door and inherited
sarcasm
Picture albums lying on the desk next to the front door
I am from Earth, I am me

Philip

I am from grass and Legos
I am from an average house, warm and inviting, it felt like home
I am from a large, old oak and a small flower
Planted precisely in the garden
I'm from having fun and working hard
From Jason and Suzy and my sisters
I'm from quiet and hard-working
From "Try your best" and "Be a good Christian"
I'm from the cross, a little church by the river
I'm from a large grassy patch
Chicken and tea
From long-distance running and hard work
I am from the fireplace and the South

"Rebel Fight Song" (to the tune of "Cheer, Cheer")

James

Cheer, cheer for ole Maryville high.

We never back down from a fight!

Send the sophomores in to win.

Don't let an injured senior in!

You want to play us? Just say when!

It's not just luck we are on ESPN.

We're not wimps, we finish them all,

We're the winners of Maryville high!

Six Word Memoirs
Haley

 At MJHS I had a blast.

Back at MJHS I learned Geometry.

"Where I'm From"
Jody Dyer

I am from hand-tied trout-luring flies and Little Debbie Swiss
Cake Rolls
From masculine creativity and feminine, abundant love
I'm from the farmhouse at the end of the holler
The Crippled Beagle Farm
Slanted floors, a crooked chimney,
And frosted paneling bedroom walls in East Tennessee winters
It felt fragile in build and strong in character
It tasted like homemade beef jerky, chicken and dumplings, fried
okra, and cornbread
It smelled like hops and barley fermenting in a one-hundred-
year-old hallway
It sounded like The University of Georgia's Larry Munson and
grownups talking and popping popcorn
After I went to bed
I'm from Nellie's puppies
Velvet paws and downy Beagle fur
A rolling pile of perfect innocence
I am from the cedar forest and Kellum Creek
From irises and Tawny day lilies
Pale grape lavender and bright orange, intricately designed,
dancing against barn wood, into water, and up steep banks

I'm from opening presents youngest to oldest, rooting for the

SEC, and gambling at Thanksgiving

From interrupters and storytellers

From athletes and educators

From strong opinions and attitudes

I'm from Donna and Scott and Wimmie and Grandmama Freddy

I'm from the romantic and respectful

I am from the resolute and resourceful

From raw intelligence

I'm from picnicking at Metcalf Bottoms

And tubing the Little River

From "Always anticipate the incompetence of others" and

"You could never do anything in this world to make us stop

loving you, Bug."

I'm from the preschool, playground, and baptismal of First

Baptist Church on the parkway in Pigeon Forge

Soulful and sweet

I'm from Columbus, Georgia and Sevier County, Tennessee

Celtic, Scots-Irish, English

A daughter of Appalachia

I'm from a Division I athlete who won the Bronze star in World

War II and his bride who, before they married, rode buses to

Atlanta every weekend to dance with soldiers

I'm from a Navy Carpenter long at sea and his bride, a hospital pastry cook, who sent him pictures of herself in long, lacy nightgowns because she missed him and wanted him to miss her

I am writer Jody Cantrell Dyer

I am teacher, "Mrs. Um"

I am my nieces' "Crazy Aunt Jody"

I am wife "Baby"

I am "Mama!"

Really, I'm just Bug

"Where I'm From"
Sherri Best McCall

I'm from Ivory soap and Jergens lotion

Matchbox cars and Crayola crayons

I'm from farmland,

Where tractors and wagons with square hay bales abound,

Crisp, fresh, it smells sweet

From hard-working southern farmers and teachers

From the smell of charcoal on the grill

And the feel of warm water on your hands as you wash the

supper dishes

I'm from fried cornbread and the smell of fresh green beans

cooking on the stove

Hominy and homemade cookies

The sweet smell of abelia bushes, peonies and clean bed sheets

hanging on the line

I'm from hybrid irises, with rich colors of the rainbow stretching

across Mamaw Great's yard

And sounds of the tall pine trees creaking and groaning as they

sway in the wind

I'm from Easter sunrise services, prayers of Thanksgiving,

Nativity scenes, and hymns of praise

From fried turkeys and "strays" on holidays,

Bare feet and corncob fights

I'm from Dean and Linda, Roe and Kathryn, Vic and Frances,
Gary and Dale
From home canning and playing in the dirt
From hugs and "I love you's"
I'm from "Your eyes will get stuck like that" and
"Shut the door, were you raised in a barn?"
From "Jesus Loves Me"
I'm from the cicadas' song and the lightnin' bugs' clear yellow
glow in the night sky
A "Best" from Carpenter's Campground and California
I'm from loose pictures and scrapbooks stacked in a plastic bin
in the closet at Dean and Linda's house
And sweet memories in mind and my heart

www.ingramcontent.com/pod-product-compliance
Lightning Source LLC
Chambersburg PA
CBHW032207190626

46810CB00019B/2107